SECOND-HAND BOOKS:
A FIRST-HAND VIEW

SECOND-HAND BOOKS: A FIRST-HAND VIEW

O.J.M. DAVIS

The Book Guild Ltd
Sussex, England

First published in Great Britain in 2001 by
The Book Guild Ltd
25 High Street
Lewes, East Sussex
BN7 2LU

Copyright © O.J.M. Davis 2001

The right of O.J.M. Davis to be identified as the author of this work has been asserted by him in accordance with the Copyright, Designs and Patents Act 1988.

All rights reserved. No part of this publication may be reproduced, transmitted, or stored in a retrieval system, in any form or by any means, without permission in writing from the publisher, nor be otherwise circulated in any form of binding or cover other than that in which it is published and without a similar condition being imposed on the subsequent purchaser.

Typesetting in Baskerville by
Acorn Bookwork, Salisbury, Wiltshire

Printed in Great Britain by
Antony Rowe Ltd, Chippenham, Wiltshire

A catalogue record for this book is available from
The British Library.

ISBN 1 85776 527 3

To my parents

CONTENTS

1	Introduction	1
2	The Book Lover	11
3	Collectors	39
4	Catalogues	51
5	Browsing in Bookshops	65
6	20-Odd Ways/20 Odd Ways ... to Annoy a Bookseller	79
7	How to Put a Customer Down	95
8	Begging, Stealing or Borrowing	103
9	The Journey of the Book	119
10	Auctions	131
11	Private Libraries	145
12	A to Z	161
13	The Second-hand Afterlife	185
14	Book Sales	197
15	The Future of the Book	215

ACKNOWLEDGEMENTS

I would like to thank the staff at The Book Guild for all their hard work; the many teachers who have inspired me, from Terry Dooley to John Fuller; Paul Blum for his interest and encouragement; and above all, Louise Walker for her innumerable insights, help with the fine-tuning, and, not least, prodigious patience.

1

Introduction

(i) What is a book for?

'A good book is the precious life-blood of a master spirit, embalmed and treasured up on purpose to a life beyond life.'
(John Milton, *Areopagitica*)

'A book, yer stupid cunt, 's not worth a fuck.'
(Tony Harrison, *v.*)

There have always been readers (if only casual ones, and not classical scholars like Milton), and there have always been non-readers (from the skinhead above to the well-educated). The former won't need to be converted, and the latter, in many cases, *can't* be. I am perhaps the last person in the world who should try. For I have been in the business of buying and selling books for many years, of treating them, in other words, as a commodity. I hear you gasping, and it does sound a little like selling one's soul. No, I am not a great writer, nor was meant to be; am an attendant parasite, one who makes his (comparatively easy) living by trafficking in the products of other people's blood, sweat and tears. And yet I read—primarily works of literature. I'd be just as well (or badly) off if I didn't; better off, in fact, by the price of a book. Do I read just to show off my knowledge, like the office worker in Robert Walser's *Helbling's*

INTRODUCTION

Story? No: how shallow you must think me. (A good reference, though, don't you think, nice and abstruse?)

Actually I will come to why I do in a minute; let's first look at the opposition. The great majority either can't or don't. If we set aside the 'can'ts' as lost souls (yes, that's 'can'ts', thank you very much), let me turn to those who merely don't. Why don't they? To some, no doubt, reading is a luxury, they're simply too busy living. They work hard, have a family to feed and clothe, payments to keep up—what can I say to them except, well, don't work so hard, don't have so many children, or indeed, any (the planet is, after all, overcrowded). If they were to say in reply that there are too many books in the world, I should have to agree with them: publishers ought to exert more quality control (naturally, I exempt my own).

But to return to the argument. There are more problematic cases; there are others who do have leisure time, plenty of it, and they choose, not to read, but to be sporty, or drink, drug and screw themselves stupid. They might say that books are fusty, out-of-date, and mostly by dead people; they're young and now and living in the real world, what are books to them? This is perhaps a convenient hypothesis; I'm putting words into their mouths. But it's a point. We live in the body as well as the mind, we're only here on a short visit, surely we should enjoy ourselves. I have arrived at a central conflict: people who live, and people who read (the crux at the heart of *A Grammarian's Funeral* by Browning). Plenty of people, of course, do both, and the best kind of experience is a synthesis of the two, a marriage of the real and the ideal. But remember, I am addressing those who live *merely* (except I'm not, because they wouldn't be reading this, now would they?). I will continue regardless. They assume that to read is to sit in a chair and be passive when one could be up and about and be active; reading about other people's lives is an excuse for not having a life oneself. (I am assuming again, you will say—but just look at that, now I'm assuming on your behalf as well as theirs, oh I can't win. But haven't you met these people? Tough—I have; in any case, this is my book, and I'll argue it any way I choose!).

INTRODUCTION

Yes, I'm told it's great fun to go abseiling down a cliff, to swim, or slalom down a slope; it must make your heart thump, and I'm sure it's very good for your lungs. But what have you got at the end of it? I know what I'd have: severe vertigo. Well, to read, say, Henry James is similarly to grapple, only to grapple with another person's mind, a devious, labyrinthine mind at that; and to dive into *The Golden Bowl* and come up again on the other side (providing you're still sane) is tremendous exercise—for the brain. It is not the plot that matters—very little happens—so much as the tortuous mental processes, the microscopic spores of feeling, belonging to the characters. So shiftingly insidious are the power games at its centre that if you sneeze you will miss something. The power resides not in anything tangible, but in what the characters do or don't know about each other, multiple layers of awareness. Nothing is spelt out for them; they have only the hieroglyphics of the human face to rely on. And for us, to gauge these subtleties is to understand how other people tick—and why: in James it's a matter of their very survival. Such invigorating gulps of cold air are the reward for attaining this interior altitude.

When we're rushing about in the cosmos we deal essentially with *ex*teriors, with places, people, things; our lives are a series of immediate surfaces with which we must interact. But a book is altogether slower, deeper, *micro*cosmic; it involves the unravelling of a skein of thought invisible to the naked eye. Sit on a train and observe ten different people reading ten different books: though they're sharing the same physical experience of sitting in a mundane, claustrophobic railway carriage, and possibly the same expression, they're all actually elsewhere, multifariously so, locked into their different mental landscapes, at best maybe even floating out into the ether, and without the doubtful benefit of drugs.

'Here we are all, by day; By night w'are hurl'd
By dreames, each one, into a sev'rall world.'
(Robert Herrick, *Dreames*)

3

INTRODUCTION

In a way, to read is to dream (and I don't mean books that provide mere Mills and Boon escapism), it's to live in a world of the imagination. And what's wrong with Mills and Boon? Plenty. Instead of being food for thought, our daily bread as it were, these production-line romances are more like blotting paper. Fluff. If that sounds élitist, then I'm afraid it is; it may not be fashionable in these egalitarian times, but I think we should always aspire to the best in everything; we're constantly surrounded by, positively drowning in the worst.

This is all very idealistic, I hear you say (I've got good ears, you'll have to admit), but isn't a book, the actual physical manifestation of it, at least of the older, leather-bound kind, rather dirty and dusty on the outside, like our own more tangible selves, an abuse, too, of trees and cows? Well, I'm all for animals and nature, but if they contribute (posthumously, in one case) to the eventual packaging of a parcel of knowledge, then they've served a useful purpose. And with such tomes it's like walking into a church, the sense of historical continuity, that other people have been here before you, handled this very book. It may be their dust you're blowing off, though you'll find it harder to remove the names that endure, stamped on bookplates within, or written out in florid dedication.

But aren't books outmoded, slow of access, twee little country lanes in an age of information highways? Not as long as people like to puzzle things out at their own pace, human, not mechanical. We have our own extraordinary technology, that of the brain; if it's not state-of-the-art, it must at least be superior to the plug-in variety—that kind wouldn't even exist without ours. (Besides, there's another thing to consider: curl-power. Can you imagine curling up on a sofa, or lying cosily in bed with a not-so-personal computer for company? You can? You do? Then I'm afraid you need medical help; all the more so if your partner happens to have a virus as well.)

The act of reading, then, is about communication. In that case, you might argue, you'd be better off talking to a friend. Well, that depends on your friends. I mean, do you know someone who can blurt out such gems as:

4

INTRODUCTION

'I peel and portion
A tangerine and spit the pips and feel
The drunkenness of things being various.'
   (Louis MacNeice: *Snow*)

Probably not, and if you do I suggest you get this friend of yours to write them down—otherwise they will be lost. A book preserves the best that human beings have to say about the universe. Life itself is a random business, evanescent, governed by chance, but the written word can knit together the threads of disparate experiences, creating order out of chaos. And the result is a one-to-one experience: you have the illusion that the writer is talking to you, and you alone, the reader at that precise moment. Books have voices, are essentially human, and whether we like it or not, so are we. We can feel less lonely reading a book, it can touch on things we've always thought or felt but never been able to put a name to, or at least not so well, succinctly. Reading is, in fact, company, not a replacement for it but an alternative kind, for it is the company of the dead as well as the living, a solidarity between individuals across the barriers of space and time. Naturally we have to be careful in our choice of companion; just as there are people in life we want to avoid, so there are authors whose voice grates on our senses, or whose point of view is alien to us. But we can learn from the enemy too. We needn't fear indoctrination. We bring our own experiences to bear on what is being said; by provoking an outcry, they can help us to clarify our attitudes. The more we read the more we discover just who is on our wavelength, who sets our minds racing, so that we can spend more time with them in future.

To some, it is true, a book will always remain offensive, a chore, associated as it might be with the forcible feeding of schooldays, the oppression of sitting still. To others a book is the opposite, as inoffensive as it is inanimate, of less practical use than a hair-dryer or a suitcase. And to the illiterate it's positively frightening. Indeed a book can be a bomb of a thing, it can explode social structures (*Das Kapital*) or religious beliefs (*The Origin of Species*), can educate us on innumerable subjects, make

INTRODUCTION

us think in new enlightened ways, or it can thrill us and chill us, make us chuckle on a dreary, drizzly day. Static we may be, but think of the locomotive effect of the words themselves, the breathless curiosity that makes you want to turn over the page of a well-told story. Books are forever; if they should stop printing them altogether, transferring their information onto CD-ROMS, people will go on collecting them, perhaps more furiously still, as they are now collecting vinyl in the age of the compact disc.

Because there are books, five centuries of them, there has to be a book trade, and one specifically geared towards the second-hand. And if—unfortunately—one has to put a book down and go out there and earn a living, one could do worse than make money out of books themselves. What am I doing, after all, but supplying a commodity that other people want, one that gives them pleasure? Some get as much pleasure from books as they do from sex, some a hell of a lot more; sublimation it may be, but isn't the sublime preferable to the ridiculous? Or put it another way: those out there who are clubbing away into the small hours and shagging each other senseless, or even just plain shopping, are probably having a good time (would they do it otherwise?), and good luck to them: but in their own way they're substituting sex for books.

Of course, as I said before, most well-adjusted, well-educated people do both, and in proportion; some, however, it has to be said, do neither. I think if Milton had to live in the modern world, he would probably have to come down off his high-minded pedestal, or at least halfway, in order to address the voice of ignorance with which I started. I think he'd have to speak more in the language of the spoken-to. I think he'd probably say:

> 'A book, yer stupid cunt, is the precious life-blood of a master spirit, embalmed and treasured up on purpose, yer piece of shit, to a life beyond life; it's not only worth a fuck, as you so eloquently put it, but to my mind, a fistful of fucks (and when's the last time you had one anyway, you son of Adam, scrap that, son of a bitch?).'

INTRODUCTION

(ii) The difference between new and second-hand books

Now the obvious answer to this question is that a new book is a pristine artefact bought in a new bookshop, and a second-hand book is a used (and often abused) product that has been turned out of its previous abode and is now lying homeless in some jaded commercial premises, waiting for its next deliverer. The age of a new book is always the same (it's a bright-eyed baby); whereas a second-hand/antiquarian item can vary between a few days to a few centuries old, from a review copy read by a journalist who sells it to supplement his meagre fee, to an incunable, a book from the birth of printing (these, alas, unlike the former, don't turn up every day). This question of appearance is at least the superficial difference between the two, though it is possible for a new book to be creased and torn (quite apart from more serious matters), and for an old book, due to some miracle of preservation in a cabinet or airtight container, to turn up mint, even if it's clearly from the world of yesteryear, with its alien typesetting and design.

The real difference, however, is more substantial. For one thing, there is no aura of mystery surrounding the value of a new book: maybe £6.99 if it's a paperback, £14.95 for a hardback novel, and £40 or more for some recondite academic treatise which will only sell to libraries and then later be remaindered for £4.99! OK, there's now no Net Book Agreement, so some shops may sell them at a little discount, between 10 and 30 per cent off, but the basic truth of the matter is that the book can't exceed a certain price. It is also, I should stress, available. You might have to order it, you might even have to import it, but if it's new it's consumer-friendly, it's sleek and clean and happy to oblige you. Clearly then, you will say, a new book is more desirable than an old one which is usually more than a little grubby and dissolute, even supposing you can get your hands on it. And what does it cost? You could scour the country and find ten different copies of the same book in similar condition all marked at different prices—from, say, £5 to £25. Nor is there a legal ceiling to its worth. What sense is there in that? What (I have to say it) decency? If no one can agree as to the

INTRODUCTION

price, what trust can you place in it? No, you can't rely on a second-hand book; apart from the fact that its value seems to be what anyone thinks he can get for it, quite often it disappears without a trace when you most need it; you could walk into a hundred bookshops, scan thousands upon thousands of titles, and still not find the one you're looking for.

And there we have it: the intrinsic superiority of the second-hand book is its very elusiveness.

I am quite aware, of course, that in this I am arguing against my own book, at least on its first appearance: it's new, it's available, why should you bother to buy it? Well, now and then you should make an exception. You never know, it might catch on, become a collector's item, and what with the first edition's short print run, a rarity indeed. After all, who should know about such things if not myself, someone with years of experience in such matters? And if you all rush out and buy it now you'll *guarantee* its rarity (not to mention a reprint or two, and further royalties for me). On the other hand, if you really do have an aversion to new books, wait till it's out of print, *then* buy it (if you can). But why am I advising you? If you're reading this now, then you've probably bought it already. Unless you're (shame on you) thumbing through it at Waterstone's. What do you think of it so far? A bit slow? Take my word for it, it gets a hell of a lot better. Go on, treat yourself, you'll concentrate much better at home. Or are you browsing perhaps in your local library? Forget it. What good is a three-week loan when you can have your own copy, read it again and again at your leisure?

Now where was I? Oh yes. Perhaps it is only the advantage of hindsight, but it seems to me that most of the best books in the world are old ones; only future generations can assess the abiding relevance of present-day publications. But even many of the classics are often (temporarily at least) out of print, if only in the particular edition you require (first editions, of course, are always so). We attach great value to them as works of literature, they are spiritually uplifting, but how much more precious they become when they are physically so elusive.

Let me be vulgar for a moment... no, please, I insist. (Female

INTRODUCTION

readers, who may find the next few lines offensive, politically if not analogically incorrect, are advised to move onto the next paragraph.) An available woman is to be prized; you call her up when you need her and she's there. But imagine a woman you caught a glimpse of some time ago, in a street, or as the old song goes, across a crowded room, and whom you've been looking for ever since. However aggravating it is, your curiosity is aroused, you won't be satisfied until you've found her. And so it is when hunting second-hand books: tracking down that anthology which you once flicked through in a hotel lounge or at a friend's house, can be infuriating; so much so that you may have resorted to 'borrowing' this book off your friend, with no intention of returning it, leaving to the latter the task of replacing it. (It goes without saying that he will also wish to replace you.) It is his turn to suffer and enjoy the thrill of the chase, a chase that might go on for years, till, just as hope is all but extinguished, suddenly, unexpectedly, perhaps in some obscure nook in the provinces—there it is!

Actually this is a mixed blessing. Some may treasure the book they've been after for so long, and hold onto it for dear life; others, oh so much sadder others, may experience the opposite. The possession, they find, is not tantamount to the pursuit, and far from appreciating it, they put it away on a shelf, forget about it, and... well, what else but go in search of another book, scores, hundreds of books they still *don't* have. (Years later perhaps, finally succumbing to a desire to read that item, they've either forgotten where it lives, or, worse, can't even reach it, tucked away as it is behind endless clutter at the back of the triple-parked topmost shelf. History repeats itself, it seems, and off they traipse in search of an accessible duplicate.) This is a sorry state of affairs, but it is also human nature. Or the nature of a collector. Whether it be books or women or butterflies (cf John Fowles), this is a person with a mission, an obsession driven by a furious need, though what makes a collector tick will vary from person to person.

For instance...

2

The Book Lover

'Do you call that normal behaviour?' asked Mrs Preston, not for the first time that morning.

Mr Preston laced up his shoes.

'I mean, do you suppose that's how decent people behave?'

He straightened his tie before the mirror.

'You obviously do,' she answered for him.

He put the morning paper into his attaché case.

'You don't contradict me, so I must assume I'm right.'

He closed his eyes. 'Must you?'

'Don't give me that.'

'All right then.' Darting them open again: 'Gillian, you're wrong.'

'I *meant* your tone. And don't be so bloody condescending.'

'I wouldn't dream of it,' he conned and descended. Taking up his case, 'Have you finished now?' he said.

'But you haven't even answered my question.'

'I've forgotten what it was,' he declared with maddening calm. 'Oh yes, was I normal?' He rolled his eyes and hunched his back. 'I should say so.'

She shook her head. 'It's just that when you introduce a friend to your husband, you don't expect him to sit there and go on reading as if nothing had happened.'

'Barking,' he concurred, opening the front door. He turned round sharply. 'But then you always knew I was different. Isn't that why you married me?' And off he went.

'You twist everything, don't you?' she called out after him. 'Heh? What do you do?'

Crossing the road, without looking back, he gave his body a sudden jerk for reply.

She slammed the door. Blinking, he continued on his way.

Mrs Preston went into the living-room and sat down. Within seconds she was in tears. Was she imagining it, or was he actually getting worse? How she cursed her bad luck—theirs. As if they hadn't had enough troubles before. Two very difficult people, she edgy and bad-tempered, he bookish and antisocial, they had met while doing their PGCE and married soon after. It had seemed the right thing to do: each of them felt that no one else would have them. It was a good idea from the financial point of view: neither of them earned enough to afford a decent place of their own; only by pooling their resources could they live comfortably. True, Mr Preston's father had money, but he might as well have been bankrupt: he was an incorrigible miser. And so they had lived together for fourteen years, by no means peacefully, but still far and away from the internecine war that had been raging recently.

The cause of the breakdown in communications was quite simple. For many years they had tried to have a child, but they had had to contend with failure. She had accused him verbally of having a low sperm count, while he had hit back by writing her a malicious poem entitled *Intimations of Infertility*. The tension between them had been considerable. Then, at the age of thirty-seven, by which time both of them had given up, she had suddenly become pregnant, and the storm clouds had temporarily lifted. If their marriage had plodded on at a snail's pace for years, there were now rapid developments in a matter of weeks. Their thwarted desires became completed actions; they moved to a bigger house to accommodate a nursery, regarding the birth of their child as a *fait accompli*. Unfortunately, it was not to be: the baby was stillborn, and both of them were thrown back into a situation far worse than before.

Initially he had taken charge, keeping his grief to himself, and pandering to his wife's needs with constant attention and an abundance of gifts. She had acknowledged his efforts with gratitude, but apparently this wasn't enough. The loss was more than a bitter disappointment; the raising and then dashing of her hopes was intolerable to her, and as time went on the wound didn't heal. The size of the house (what with the extra room a constant reminder) preyed on her hypersensitive nature, yet it was her idea not to move: the room was a symbol of hope, of the possibility of children. Often when alone she would sit there, take off her blouse, tug at a nipple with her fingers, and start whispering endearments, as she imagined herself suckling a baby. Meanwhile her husband, realising that there were serious limits to his consideration, cut himself off from her more and more, and was to be found propped in his favourite armchair of an evening, reading till late. His increasing neglect exacerbated her condition; while her escalating tendency to nag only further confirmed him in his ways. They stopped making love.

At this juncture Mrs Preston's best friend, Cath Ogilvy, learning of their troubles, recommended that they visit Marriage Guidance. Mr Preston, already resigned to the worst, was against the idea, but in order to please his wife agreed to go.

During the first session the woman counsellor dwelt on the theme of fostering: had they considered it? Mr Preston said he refused to consider it, and there was an end of the matter.

During the second session she drummed into them the essential need to keep on trying for another child, and on no account to give up hope. Mr Preston said it was hopeless.

But this time his wife interceded. It *had* occurred to them, she said, if not in open discussion, at least in little hints of the eyes, and hesitations of speech; they had been afraid to broach the subject, as a second failure would finish them. Mr Preston nodded that it was so. His wife patted his hand. Seizing her opportunity, the counsellor asked if they knew any better way of coping with their grief. They replied that they did not.

But the renewal of sexual activity—let alone the conception of another child—was not so simple as they supposed. To his considerable embarrassment, Mr Preston found that he could not sustain enough interest. His wife, clinging desperately to the last vestiges of hope, responded badly: she railed at him. And the more self-conscious he became, the shorter the measure he gave.

'Call yourself a man!' she yelled after his seventh successive failure.

Her anger made him angry; and indeed this direct attack on his masculinity had the desired effect. The next time they went to bed he became intensely aroused—which was a pity, for she did not. It was the turn of her body to express their anxiety. After several weeks of this he had had enough: he announced that there was to be no further attempt at intimacy. But she couldn't accept this. Perseverance would pay dividends, she said. He wouldn't listen. And when she started pleading with him he maintained his stubbornness, turning his back on her, and immersing himself once more in a book. Last night had been typical of this new outbreak of hostilities. After introducing a friend from the women's group she had joined, he had merely looked up, given a perfunctory nod, and resumed his reading as if he had done all that was required.

* * * * *

It was now, in fact, that his lifelong interest in books turned into an obsession. He already possessed some five hundred titles arranged along shelves in the hall and living-room. But far from sitting down to read these, he now preferred to go out on Saturday afternoons and buy several new volumes to add to his collection. There was nothing alarming about this; however, after a relatively quiet period of weekend buying, Mrs Preston watched her husband come in from work one Monday evening, carrying not only his black attaché case, but a carrier bag too, containing yet another batch of fresh purchases.

'Couldn't you at least have waited until the weekend?'

'What does it matter *when* I buy them?' he snapped impatiently. 'Anyway you made such a fuss last Saturday about how I hardly said a word to you—'

'As if I didn't have every right to expect—'

'Well then, now I'm buying books in my lunch hour—in my own time, that is.'

'But if that means you're not eating properly...'

'My God, there's always something, isn't there?'

'Just because I show a bit of concern...'
'No, Gillian, it's so that you can have something to complain about.'
'But I wasn't,' she insisted, stamping her foot with fury.
'That statement in itself...'
Then he picked up the bag of books and walked into the living-room.

He thought he'd been perfectly reasonable, though he was aware that there were always two sides to an argument, his wife might feel seriously neglected, and it was just possible his supercilious tone might cause offence. When Saturday came round, in fact, he spent several hours making it up to her: driving her into town so that she could do some shopping, watching her faff around with apparently limitless pairs of shoes, buying her cakes at a patisserie. He was excessively considerate, sarcastically so; the day was all hers. Almost. He couldn't help just popping into a neighbouring bookshop and spending forty minutes (and as many pounds) inside.

Things continued like this for months. Sometimes it occurred to him he was being complacent, that his wife couldn't create her own interests as he could, but her persistent nagging had rendered him insensitive. The prickings of guilt grew less and less frequent, his saccharine moods of sweetness all but disappeared, and the realm of quiet vindictiveness reigned supreme. Books were his one compensation for an empty life; unfortunately he remained hers.

Mr Preston became a familiar figure to the booksellers of the Charing Cross Road. Tramping up and down there several times a week, stooping beneath the weight of books already bought, his eagle eyes glued to the temptations in their windows, they bent over backwards to invite his custom. They encouraged him with substantial discounts; they managed to get on first-name terms with him; one sycophantic dealer even plied him with coffee as he browsed among his stock.

Such was the extent of Mr Preston's collecting that he had soon run out of shelf-space in the living-room; he made some preliminary enquiries of a handyman to install some new ones in the nursery.

'But you can't do that,' his wife exclaimed one evening, when he had finally summoned up the courage to mention it.

'And why ever not?' he coolly replied, as if he hadn't anticipated trouble.

'Because... because...'

'Do we have any other use for that room?'

'Yes. It's... our baby's room.' He looked at her. 'But there's always a chance... I'm not even forty yet.'

'That's no longer the issue, is it?'

'It was your idea to stop.'

'But what's the point in kidding ourselves, Gillian? Why keep these wretched dreams alive?'

She wanted to say that dreams were all she had now, but was aware how pathetic this would sound; and wasn't there pathos in his words too? His anger was an attempt at concealment, but actually it laid things bare: he was angry with both of them: '*our*selves', he had said. She began to see that this newly acquired fanaticism was just his own way of dealing with failure.

'At least we could try,' she persisted.

'We tried for fourteen years,' he said, with increasing exasperation. 'Don't you think that's enough?'

'But even if I am dreaming, as you say, we could always...' (she hesitated—she knew it would annoy him) '... look into fostering.'

'We've discussed that before,' he answered curtly.

'We did not; you dismissed it before I could get a word in.'

'But if one party is completely against it... Look. The only child I'm going to have is my child. Not someone else's. OK?'

'The usual refrain. Your books, your child. If I'm prepared to—'

'Then that's your affair. If you don't like it, you know what you can do.'

At this she turned away and crumpled into a heap. For a moment he felt ashamed, bitterly so, but he wouldn't admit it openly: it was his stubborn streak again.

Three days later the handyman came round and got to work on the nursery.

Mr Preston, who doubled as maths teacher and careers coordinator, was spending his free periods interviewing. One boy said he wanted to run a bookshop. Naturally warming to the theme, he asked him a lot of questions, till he realised he had misheard: 'run a book', the boy must have said. Mr Preston was appalled. But the day sped swiftly by, what with its myriad young faces, ambitions.

Mrs Preston was at home, on one of her weeks off from supply teaching. She found it impossible to concentrate on anything: the interminable woodworking sounds coming from the nursery gave her a migraine; she felt she was being sawn in half. And as the leaden day wore on, the futility of her life was hammered home with each nail. When at last the handyman had finished, she gave him a cheque already made out by her husband; despite her offhand manner, he thanked her, then left the house, preserving in his mind an image of red-rimmed eyes and grey-stained cheeks.

That evening Mr Preston came home and went straight to the nursery. He rubbed his hands as he examined the scene before him. All he saw was the finished product—five new shelves on either side of the fireplace—not the sweat that went into it, *hers* above all. He took a few books out of a carrier bag that had sat there waiting, placed them lovingly on one of the topmost shelves, and then stood back, tilting his head, to admire.

'Ah don't you look wonderful!' he cried.

Mrs Preston had entered the room quietly behind him.

'It may surprise you to know that some husbands say that to their wives when they come home.'

'Oh hello, dear,' he replied mock-chirpily, choosing to ignore her remark. He crossed the room to take her hand. 'A fine job, eh?'

'An expensive one. And something we haven't talked about is where you're getting the money to feed this ridiculous obsession.'

'Why is it so?' he challenged indignantly—and tactically; he had avoided her question.

'For one thing, you'll never have time to read all these books.'

'I'm not dead yet, you know.'

'That's your opinion.'

He pursed his lips. 'Why don't you find an interest of your own?'

She followed this thought to its furthest extremity. 'Another husband, for instance?'

'I'm still here, aren't I? I haven't deserted you.' She laughed contemptuously. 'Well, I'm sorry if you take it like that,' he huffed, putting on his best impersonation of henpecked innocence. 'As for the money...' he went on, now strategically reverting to the former issue, if only to evade the latter.

'Don't back out of it,' she read him only too well.

'You *asked* me about the money,' he raised his voice, inwardly marvelling at his nerve. 'Since apparently you need reminding, I put a little aside in case we had a family.'

'But all of it went on the new house,' she put in suspiciously.

It was enough to spoil his flow.

'Well... some of it... yes,' he conceded, speaking slowly to give himself time to think. It was no use: she wouldn't miss such an opportunity: he had tied himself in knots.

'You mean there's more than you said,' she pounced. 'Christ, you're as bad as your bloody father.'

'How dare you?' he raised his voice again, only this time it was all bluster. 'All I mean is there's enough to afford the odd luxury.'

Her mouth opened, but nothing came out; she wouldn't let it. She had caught herself out too, several times, that awful plaintive note, and despaired to think the whining old woman was her.

'Go on,' he said. 'You were going to say that I never buy you anything.'

She didn't answer, didn't try to defend herself; but her silence only made him more triumphant.

'And now you can say "but I didn't say it", can't you?' he mocked. Then came up close. 'You thought it though.'

She considered this. 'Yes. You're quite right. I'm afraid I can't help my thoughts.' She bowed her head.

He was astonished: it was a gesture he'd never seen before. Could it be surrender? Nor had there been a trace of phoney martyrdom about it; it was only too genuine. She was sorry, and now that she was, he saw that he was the one who ought to be. He made overtures.

'Please...' he began.

'I don't want gifts, Gordon,' she stalled him, her eyes filmy, and searching his with a deep sadness; 'all I want is... a bit of attention. Is that so pathetic?'

'Of course not,' he was forced to reply; but for once he meant it.

'I think it is,' she said, and winced in disgust.

That evening he was more attentive in the course of a few hours than he had been during the whole of the last six weeks. He helped her with the casserole—an immensity; took her out to the local for an after-dinner drink; fussed over her with his handkerchief when she spilled a drop of brandy on her blouse; put his coat round her as they walked back through the goose-pimply September night; and, as the crowning conclusion to the evening, made love to her for the first time in many months.

Perhaps this might have initiated a new period of harmony in their lives, perhaps it was always going to be a temporary reconciliation; but something happened three days later that separated them once more. At the age of seventy-nine, Mr Preston's father died. The news was no surprise (he had been ill for some time), but it was nonetheless a shock; and in the same way as he had retreated into himself when his baby died, so now the pattern set in again. Mrs Preston, too, as was her wont, clung to her husband in this time of distress; she was upset because he was, and did everything she could to support him. He wanted to grieve alone, though, to shut her out once more, and so they were back where they started. Worst of all perhaps, the old man had left a staggering six-figure sum; and when all the business of the funeral and death duties and the selling off of property was accomplished, Mr Preston started putting the money to use.

After a lull of nearly four months—a lull which made the renewal of the habit even more extreme—he went out buying books again. And not just any old books; not just ordinary works of fiction, history or travel. Mrs Preston looked on with bemusement, as her husband came home one Monday laden with bags, and proceeded to pull out several volumes *bound in leather*.

Her voice was shrill. 'Not bindings!'

'Don't you like them?' He deliberately interpreted her criticism as an aesthetic one. 'It was going through father's books again that did it; I never realised he kept old bindings up in the attic.'

'Of course—out of anybody's reach. And you'll end up the same.'

He blew a raspberry. 'So much for your support.'

'But what about the...?' She faded out.

'Cost?' he smiled.

She stood there quietly for a few minutes, but as he continued about his work, arranging his new purchases along the shelves in the nursery, and blithely ignoring her, she couldn't help it, she regretted it before she spoke, but speak she must.

'Why do you have to... ruin everything?'

'I don't know what you mean,' he replied absently, examining a book which had a loose page. 'Blast! This vignette's coming away. Gillian, could you be a lamb and get me the glue?'

'Get it yourself!'

'And the boards have got detached,' he went on, as if mumbling to himself, 'I should have checked it more carefully before I—'

'For heaven's sake, Gordon! Is our marriage of no importance to you?' She hesitated before adding: 'You'd rather fondle a book than fondle me.'

'Don't be vulgar. Just because I'm bringing a bit of culture into our lives.'

'What good is that if you lock yourself away and never discuss anything? Not with me, not with anybody. Your friends have all given up on you, and if you're not careful, I'll do the same.'

His only reaction was to fetch the glue.

'And since that doesn't seem to pose a threat to you I'll stay with you instead, and make your life a misery, as you've made mine.'

The next day she consulted her best friend Cath again, and asked her what she would do in this situation. She was typically matter-of-fact.

'You could always leave him,' she said, lighting a cigarette. 'That might earn his respect. He might even find he needed you.'

'But I haven't got your strength,' Mrs Preston replied, banging the table in frustration. As her friend raised her eyebrows, 'Mentally,' she added.

Cath Ogilvy had had the gumption to walk out on three husbands (infidelity, feet, violence) and now lived with a much younger man.

'Is there no other way to make him see sense?'

'Have an affair.'

'You know that's not for me.'

'I suppose you could always compromise,' said Cath, with an expression of mild distaste. 'Has it never occurred to you to share his interest?'

'Of course. In the old days, in fact, we did talk about books.'

'There you are.'

'But it's not an interest, Cath. It's tearing us apart.'

'Well, you did ask my opinion.' She flicked off some ash impatiently as if it were the problem itself.

'I know.' And she took her friend's hand. 'Perhaps you're right.'

That very evening, when her husband had walked in and proceeded to unload his daily booty, she followed him into the nursery. He took no notice of her. She stood there preparing her lines. She must inject her voice with enthusiasm.

'What have you bought today then?' she made herself say, but the words spilled out with an unnatural jauntiness.

Turning round with a smile, 'Darling,' he greeted her affectionately.

He had guessed she was trying to iron things out. Her attempt was extremely clumsy. But in his own way he craved for peace—on his terms, that is.

'Lots of things. To begin with, there's this delightful edition of Dryden's *Poetical Works*, Victorian of course—'

'I didn't know you liked him,' she observed, making an effort at discussion.

'I don't. Still one must have him. I say Victorian, but as you can see it's been re-backed within the last ten years.'

'Oh? How can you tell?'

She plied him with questions to flatter his interest; maybe they could then change the subject.

'You get to know these things after a while,' he returned in as blasé a manner as possible. He liked giving the impression of superior knowledge; actually the bookseller had told him. 'Some might say the binding was a little tawdry,' he continued, 'but personally I prefer something recent and solid to one that's old and falling apart.'

'I quite agree with you,' she smiled.

'I thought you'd understand,' he smiled back. But it was he who didn't. He thought she was enjoying the benefit of his wisdom, whereas it was his pomposity that amused her. An obsessive, he lacked the ability to look at himself from the outside, to compass another's ironic detachment. 'Anyway, what else? Ah yes, this three-volume Shakespeare, tree-calf, in lovely condition; a fine book on angling, 1794, half morocco, with beautiful steel engravings, only slightly foxed,' he went on in his best esoteric manner. 'Oh, and the smell,' he sniffed it lovingly.

She felt rather offended at this; she had put on her favourite perfume especially.

As he offered it to her, 'A bit musty,' she wrinkled her nose.

'But it's history, Gillian. Do you know, the person who first owned this was living in the time of the French Revolution, the *sans-culottes*—'

'It makes you think, doesn't it?' she cut him short: his accent was hateful. 'Forgive me for saying so, darling,' she added, 'but what can you want with a book on fishing? I mean, you're not likely to read it, are you?'

'These books aren't meant for that. They're for dipping into, or at the very least for display.'

'I see.' She checked her irritation. 'If it gives you pleasure, I suppose...'

He resumed his inventory. 'I almost forgot. Do you know what this is? Wait for it—this is the first edition, the very first, mind, of Arnold's *Culture and Anarchy*...'

The conversation, no, the lecture, lasted another twenty minutes. By this time Mrs Preston was feeling utterly worn out;

she had shown an interest in her husband's collecting, but all it amounted to was to condone the obsession, encouraging him to expatiate at horrendous length.

'I'd better get on with the dinner,' she eventually announced, as casually as possible, not wishing to suggest she might be bored.

'OK. And I'll push on with this. You know, there's only these three and a half shelves left. I think I'll have to get that chap in again to put some up in the bedroom.'

It was all the more devastating for being so offhand. Any idea of meeting him halfway ... As for his crass attempt at culture, it hardly kept anarchy at bay: the rage in her alone was ungovernable.

'You will not compromise, will you?'

'But where else can I have them? On the roof? Or perhaps you'd prefer I turned the bathroom into a library?'

'Isn't it enough that you've desecrated the nursery? You've destroyed every... every...'

'Illusion?' he supplied with glee. 'Isn't it about time you faced reality?'

'The way you do, I suppose? By burying my head in a pile of filthy old moth-eaten tomes that no one has ever read, let alone...' (and here she had to break off for a humiliating sneeze) '...dusted. It's revolting. And now you want to inflict your perversity—'

'But I have every right to have shelf-space—'

'It's me you're shelving,' she pointed at herself. 'Can't you see it? My God, you're a swine.'

'And it's living with you that's made me one.'

The atmosphere changed abruptly. She went ominously quiet. For the first time he felt scared, of what he wasn't sure, but enough to make him swallow, which in turn made his cheeks redden, for he was convinced the sound had carried in the silence. He was even more alarmed when she spoke, slowly, with extreme emphasis, and with lips pressed quiveringly together. Like the lid over a cauldron, wobbling, precarious.

'I don't know if I can forgive you for that. The only thing I tell myself is that, deep inside, you're as unhappy as I am.

Another *illusion* if you like...' (she sneered at the reminder) '...but it's all that keeps me going. You see, I can't believe you're simply cruel; it would make a travesty of the last sixteen years.'

'But Gillian, I never intended—'

'So please, Gordon, don't put up shelves in the bedroom; I wouldn't like it at all.'

And with that she left the room, went into the kitchen, and prepared the dinner. He judged the intensity of her state of mind by the degree to which it was burnt. They ate in complete silence.

The words seemed to have taken some effect, for a week went by, and nothing was said about shelves being put up in the bedroom. But a few days later Mrs Preston came home from teaching, went into the bathroom to have a wash, and, as she reached for her towel from the rail, received the shock of her life to see, suspended from the wall above it, several new shelves of timber.

'You *cannot* put shelves in the bathroom,' she challenged him as soon as he was over the threshold.

He smiled. 'Well, you didn't want them in the bedroom, dear, and they can't just sit about on the floor indefinitely. Let's call it a... compromise.'

'You bastard! You're doing this deliberately.'

'But I don't understand,' he said with unconvincing innocence. His inveterate obstinacy, as always at loggerheads with her more importunate nature, made him unpleasant.

'You can't! You can't!' she cried, in full percussion now. 'No one in their right mind...'

'Well, I'm different, aren't I? Now it's shelves here, or it's shelves in the bedroom. Decide.'

At this point she marched out of the bathroom, could be heard rummaging about in the kitchen, and soon came storming back. He gasped. She was wielding a hammer.

'What the hell are you doing?' he tried to restrain her.

'Since you don't seem to understand...' she said, and then broke off talking in order to lay into a shelf.

'Don't you dare! Stop that at once!'

'Keep away!' she shrieked, 'or I'll use it on you.'

'You haven't got the guts.'

She glared at him; he froze for a moment. She didn't speak, she wouldn't reassure him; she wanted to see fear in his eyes first.

'Have you?' he added, with what sounded like considerable uncertainty.

It was enough. 'You're quite right,' she laughed, 'I haven't. But you'd better stand back, or you'll get splinters in your eyes.'

She had damaged one of the shelves irreparably before he could wrest the hammer from her.

He went away muttering under his breath. She herself was rather proud.

But the clash of wills didn't end there. Apparently she underestimated even his nerve; he would not accept defeat. The next day there was a ring at the door. It was Tim, the handyman.

'What do you want?' fired Mrs Preston with unashamed hostility.

He was tentative. 'It's about some... shelves?' he began.

'Shelves!' she screeched. 'Don't talk to me about...'

It wasn't as if he'd said 'sex'. 'But your husband—'

'I know,' she said, with a maniacal glint in her eye; 'oh I know, believe me.' Then she shut the door in his face.

'Thank God I'm not hitched,' he muttered, walking away.

When Mr Preston arrived home that night, he went straight into the bedroom, and, seeing that no shelves had been put up, and that his wife was padding about with unusual complacency, confronted her.

'You didn't let him in, did you?'

'A brilliant deduction.'

He turned his back on her.

'And what are you going to do about it?' she followed him out. Then stopped in her tracks. She knew he would do *something*.

The next morning, a Tuesday, she was surprised to see him leave the house without the customary attaché case, and dressed, of all things, in dungarees. She only twigged what was happening when he returned, half an hour later, armed with some planks of timber, and assorted packets of nails and screws.

'Oh my God!' she cried, as he barged past her, through the hall, and on into the bedroom. 'It's my room too!'

'You had your choice,' he said over his shoulder. Plonking the materials down: 'And if you don't like it, you can sleep on the sofa.'

Once again the sound of hammering and sawing could be heard echoing through the house. She crouched in the corner of the kitchen, her forefingers stopping her ears, her teeth gritted, her lips mouthing obscenities, and weeping, weeping all the time. He had broken her will. Sheer persistence had beaten her. He was even prepared to sacrifice a day at work—work he took quite seriously—in order to prove who was master. She hated his will to win. She hated his books. They were no longer mere artefacts (had they ever been such?), they were a weapon used against her, supplanting the bond that she and her husband had shared. It wasn't enough for him that they had swarmed in their hordes across the desert of the nursery; now they must invade this final sanctuary, watching over those future intimacies to which she still clung.

When he had finished his work, three of the four walls of the bedroom had shelves affixed to them. Only the wall above the bed was free.

Later that afternoon she roused herself out of her crestfallen state, and paid another visit to Cath. Her friend didn't so much advise as command her.

'Leave him! Gillian, there *is* nothing else. I mean, you can't possibly still love him.'

'I don't know. I hate him, that's for sure; as to the other ... He's so damn strong; and after all our years together—'

'You must make a fresh start. There are no children to hold you down.'

'And that's the plus side?'

'There's a spare room—now please make use of it.'

'Bless you, but I couldn't intrude.'

'I'll take it as a personal insult if you don't.'

The next three weeks saw Mrs Preston on the verge of

collapse. She stayed on at the house, partly because she was afraid to leave, but also because she refused to surrender in full. When she was working, she found sufficient distraction during the day; when she wasn't, she would drift like a zombie through the house, wondering how to accommodate the hours. In the mornings she shopped and dusted and hoovered and sewed; in the afternoons she took to watching escapist Hollywood oldies on the box: slushy romances with cool-looking heroines wearing nylons in the tropics; or manic musicals where complete strangers burst simultaneously into song. Something wasn't right, she knew, when *Singin' in the Rain* failed to invigorate her—the 'Make 'Em Laugh' routine made her frown.

She tried new things. She went to pubs with women from her group, women who were lonely or divorced, and got into tight corners with smoky, elbow-nudging, beer-gutted men. She performed superfluous tasks. One bruised grey morning, to cheer herself up, she convinced herself that the bathroom ought to be painted pink, when its soft cream walls had always pleased her before. There was only one thing she wouldn't do... until the frantic Friday came when she resorted even to that. She had never felt so ashamed. Gordon must never know. For Mrs Preston had picked up—she still couldn't credit it—one of her husband's books. Worse: she had read it from cover to cover.

She stayed in the living-room most of the day, only entering the bedroom last thing at night. She wouldn't be forced out. Invariably, when she went in, her husband was standing in worship before his shrine of books, with such a pious expression she half-expected him to genuflect; or he was stretched out at his offensive ease on the double bed, perusing one volume after another, grunting away with laconic approval.

There was one development only. No longer did he come home weighed down with carrier bags. Mrs Preston was foolish: in a myopic moment she had seen this as cause for celebration. Once more she had underestimated her husband. For a new era had begun—the era of the box. When the first van had drawn up, and a man in uniform had come tottering towards the door beneath his load, she had caught her breath. But soon she was used to it. Boxes in the morning, boxes in the afternoon; boxes from book clubs, boxes from shops; boxes even from private addresses. Their home had become a storage depot, and there was nothing she could do about it. Books had gnawed through the house like termites; she watched with terror as the last precious inches of shelf-space were being eaten away. With each new arrival she signed away the last scraps of her marriage, yet she hardly ever alluded to the matter now, or made more than cursory remarks on any subject. In return her husband seldom spoke to her, merely acknowledging her presence with a greeting, or glancing up from what he was reading with a nod. She was an acquaintance then, for this was how he had treated her women friends in the past. Once a week, perhaps in token of his gratitude, he took her out for an Indian meal; but if the food itself was hot, the aura surrounding them was glacial. They received curious looks from waiters and customers alike.

This state of affairs continued until the day when, the latest parcel having arrived, the final shelf-space was filled in, and Mr Preston proudly announced that he had finished his collecting.

Almost.

'Of course, there is room for just one more shelf above the bed,' he added, without the usual uncertainty.

'I see.'

'But when I've put that up, darling, it really will be the end.'

And after the nightmare Mrs Preston had that very night she could only agree: it really was the end.

The next morning she asked with apparent good humour: 'Are you fixing the shelf today?'

'Yes, this afternoon, I think. Why do you ask?'

'Oh, no reason. Nothing that need concern you anyway.'

He failed to perceive the ambiguity of her statement, and as the day wore on was so busy that he didn't even notice his wife flitting to and fro about the house, packing up her most essential things, and closing the front door quietly behind her. He had no idea she'd gone at all until, at six o'clock that evening, he found a curious note in the kitchen:

'Your dinner is in the oven, but despite all your efforts,

my head is not. I am taking it, and my possessions, elsewhere.

P.S. I have put the joint on 4; I hope the meat is not too leathery.'

Puzzled by a strange smell, he donned the oven-gloves, pulled out the grid, and looked into the tray. He was furious. In it were the charred remains of one of his most treasured bindings.

His first reaction was to view the whole thing as a joke, albeit in bad taste. He had never thought his wife would have the courage to walk out on him; moreover he couldn't think where she'd go. Her parents were dead, and her only brother, to whom she'd never been close, lived abroad. But when night came and she didn't return, followed by another evening alone, he realised that she was serious. He remembered her friend Cath, and supposed that she had gone to stay there, with what plans he couldn't guess. He resented this woman's influence; he felt that she had poisoned Gillian against him. Still the house was quiet for once. Not that there had been fireworks for the last few weeks—his wife had apparently admitted defeat—but she had seemed to dangle about her a fuse that needed only one small incident to ignite it. And there it was: the shelf that hung over the bed (already filled up with books). Was it really that bad? he thought. Did it take on some extra-special significance for her? One could never tell with women. Still, things hadn't blown up in his face; he thought he preferred this veil of silence, even if there was something more than a little sinister about not being aware of his wife's movements.

Quiet: the house had never been so quiet. And while Mr Preston enjoyed the novelty at first, after a week of it he couldn't help noticing that it was a little *too* quiet. He would come home from work, at a less sprightly pace than usual, grab a greasy Chinese take-away, and then settle down to a few chapters of an old travel book about Tibet. But instead of relaxing in his velvet armchair, and taking in the vicarious pleasures of bracing Himalayan altitudes, sojourns at Buddhist monasteries, and processions of the Dalai Lama, he couldn't escape to these exotic lands at all, but felt rooted at the heart of mundane suburbia.

He could no longer get comfortable. He would look up from the page, scan his immediate surroundings, and become prey to a stifling claustrophobia, as the books that lined the shelves on all sides seemed to hem him in. Small sounds frightened him. If a cat mewed, or a door creaked, his pulse would beat faster, he would find it strangely difficult to breathe. He kept telling himself it was a morbid reaction, that this was what he had always wanted. He even tried to prove it. Restless, he would prowl about from room to room, go over to a shelf, pick a volume out at random, and pause at a favourite woodcut of a woman reaping, or a hand-coloured drawing of an orchid, delighting in the knowledge that these books were among his personal possessions.

But as the days went by this ritual took on something like desperation: the woman reaping seemed more and more an artificial replacement for his wife; the orchid far less desirable than the real bunches of cyclamen and pale blue irises that sprouted out of vases in every room. Or used to: they had wilted in his wife's absence. And now that she was gone her touch—a touch he hadn't recognised before—was missing from everything. He longed to see her camisole draped over a bedroom chair; to prick up his ears again at kitchen cracklings and bubblings; to catch a whiff of bath oil, talc or other odours of reassurance.

The house became leaden. Dust filled the empty rooms. Only now did he realise that in collecting almost three thousand books he had walled himself inside a fortress, enclosed himself in a private world that no other being could share. He had expanded his consciousness, but in doing so he had become as dry and shrivelled as a faded parchment. He had never grieved properly for the loss of his baby, he had almost forgotten that his father was dead, and worst of all he knew he could not grieve now, could not go to his wife and admit he'd been wrong, for he was the same obstinate man as ever, doomed by his own intransigence.

Two nights later, as he lay tossing and turning, the shelf

above the bed came crashing down, the timber catching the side of his head, the book spines glancing off his collar-bone, shoulder blades and solar plexus. He crawled over to the telephone. The paramedics found him semi-conscious. He was muttering something about retribution.

* * * * *

'I'm all right,' said Mr Preston, as he sat up in his bed at the hospital, recovering from concussion. He didn't want to give away that he was shaken.

'You are a fool,' replied his wife, who had come as soon as she had heard. 'You might have hurt yourself.'

He shook his head: whether at her suggestion or his own conduct, she couldn't be sure.

'You must admit it was going a bit far,' she thrust.

'I don't know what you mean,' he parried with surly disingenuousness.

'I can believe that.' But she didn't. She too was lying. She knew he wasn't as indifferent as he appeared. He was being too defensive for that. And his eyes refused to meet hers. She could bide her time, however. All she said was, 'You and your books,' as if the situation were faintly humorous, and not crucial for the preservation of her marriage.

There was a pause. An old man coughed in the next bed.

'Do you know if any were damaged?' he asked suddenly, and looking at her for the first time. She was sure it was a bluff, this casualness, but she played along with it all the same.

'For goodness' sake, you might have been killed.'

He shrugged; and then, on further consideration: 'I suppose I shouldn't have put a shelf above the bed.'

'Oh you suppose so, do you?'

She kept her eyes fixed on him. His remained averted. Somehow she must break through his defences. Perhaps silence would do the trick: her lips were tightly sealed. But the presence of other people didn't help. She could see that old man out of the corner of her eye: he was scratching away at his privates. The last thing she wanted to do was laugh, she didn't even find it funny, but it was just because she knew she mustn't that she nearly did. If only she were alone with her husband. She tried not to be distracted. Her eyes remained steady.

'I...' he began at last, without looking up.

It was a single, hesitant word, but to her it was an enormity. Surely it expressed a complete change of attitude. Yet he seemed anxious to take it back. She wouldn't let him. For her, this was the beginning or the end. She directed all her concentration towards willing him to speak. Nothing further was forthcoming. She must draw him out then, convert that one dribbling word into a torrent.

'You were saying?' she prompted.

'I... can't help thinking,' he went on, still not looking at her, '...that it was a sign.'

'How do you mean?'

She thought she knew exactly what he meant, but he must say it himself.

He gave her a searching glance; then his eyes dropped again.

'I don't know,' he said vaguely.

He must be shaken, he was thinking, to have admitted even that much. Had he gone too far? For he understood her game. He knew she would be upon him now. But there was a difference: he didn't know whether he could resist her.

'Please go on,' she said, as gently as possible, not wanting to press him too hard, yet refusing to let the opportunity pass.

'Well... well...' (his arms moved restlessly about the blanket) '...you know, a... *sign*...'

She went back to playing innocent. She just looked at him questioningly.

'I mean... the accident... it was like... fate, don't you see? It was the very shelf, Gillian, the one that... well, made you go away.'

'Oh it's just a coincidence,' she said, not wanting to triumph over him: that was what *he* would have done. In any case, she knew she must proceed with subtlety: being who he was, he would now contradict her. There was a third reason, too, but she tried to forget that for the moment.

He shook his head. 'No, that's what tipped the balance.' He looked at her again. 'For me too, it seems.'

Her pulse was racing. She had him: she knew she did. But she mustn't spoil it now. She must pretend not to understand.

'Sorry?'

'Being alone... it made me think, Gillian.' He bit his lip: this was terribly hard, harder than anything he had had to do in his life. If he wasn't so weak, so drained of his ... But then, was it such a bad thing to admit a mistake? It was difficult enough. Unless that was just his way of excusing himself.

'I thought a lot about you,' he went on. 'That basically I... I...'

Any second now and *she* would need treatment.

'And then this business of the shelf... I suppose it was the final straw.'

'But what exactly?' she pressed harder.

'It's... it's...' (his fingers were clawing the blanket now) '...made me realise how much I need you.'

She stared at him for a long time without saying anything. Her face went completely red. He wondered at it and waited for a reaction. For one awful moment he thought she would choke on his need, spit it back in his face. Now that his was confessed, she might more easily relinquish her own. After a minute, however, she leaned slowly, deliberately forward, put her arm round his neck, and kissed him.

'Thank you.'

The old man clapped mischievously.

'I feel so guilty too...' added Mr Preston: since the unspeakable had been spoken...

She, on the contrary, had already heard enough. 'Don't,' she cut him short.

He noticed that she was trembling, there were tears in her eyes, the overflow, he supposed, from a bath of emotion; for surely they were reconciled.

But it didn't abate.

'You don't know how far you've driven me. You'll never know.'

He couldn't understand her. 'I'll make it up to you,' he went on. 'I promise.'

She shook her head.

'Won't you forgive me then?'

'Of course,' she said dismissively.

But could she forgive herself? It had taken her years to get him to say he needed her; would it take her as long to make a confession of her own? He *didn't* know how far he'd driven her: after hoping against hope for a week to hear from him, after damning him to hell for his obstinate nature, finally she had gone round to the house one afternoon for more of her belongings, and... pausing in front of those books above the bed—the bed that had been theirs—in a mad fit of resentment she had grabbed hold of a screwdriver.

And set to work. *Loosening the shelf.*

Naturally there were things she could say in her defence. She had hovered there for an hour in an agony of mind as to whether to tighten the screws again; in any case, she had hoped to frighten rather than to harm him, for the shelf might easily have fallen when he wasn't underneath; either way, she had paid for it through insomnia. But she knew that when she put it into words she wouldn't be able to argue so clearly; she would falter as she watched his changing expression. The end of yet another reconciliation. For there was no reason why he should listen to her excuses. It was shameful.

Was it better then, she now asked herself, to live with her guilty secret and keep her husband, than to divulge it and thereby lose him? The shelf might have fallen on him anyway; he himself believed it, and it was fitting it should be so. She had dreamed such a calamity in the first place. And yet as he looked into her eyes so trustingly, convinced in his heart of hearts that they were together again, she knew they weren't unless she spoke, they could never make a clean slate of things unless she was as honest as he had been.

'Oh God!' she cried out loud, gripped in the vice of her dilemma.

'Whatever's the matter?'

'There's something I haven't told you,' she forced out, 'something that might destroy us.'

'You must tell me then,' he said quite calmly, his mind, however, conjuring monstrosities.

'Your accident...' she began.
'Yes?'
'... it... wasn't.'
He strained to understand.
'What I'm... trying to say... I was so angry with you that I...'
'Go on!' he insisted.
'Well, I came to the house one day when you were out, and at the sight of all those books (oh Gordon, I couldn't help it) I went to the kitchen...'
But just as she was working up momentum, she caught a glimpse of the old man grimacing, his tongue lolling obscenely out at her. It was enough. She couldn't go on.
'Just ignore him,' said her husband.
'I can't! I can't!'
'You must,' he grabbed her fiercely. 'You went to the house and—' She shook her head. 'You went to the kitchen...' She wouldn't take her cue: she was shivering now. 'Kitchen...'
At last she stared at him. Her eyes were like planets.
'And took out a screwdriver,' she finished. The 'screw' came out relishingly; the 'driver' tailed off into dismal regret. '*Now* do you understand?'
He didn't speak. He didn't move. She supposed he understood.
'It might not have hurt you...' she began, but the words were muffled: she had sunk her head onto his left shoulder.
He didn't speak.
'I must have been crazy!'
He didn't move.
'Tell me what you're thinking,' she said, looking up at him. His eyes were fixed impassively on the opposite wall. What demons did he see?
Silence. If only he would speak: if it was the end, it was the end, but...
'I'm thinking...' His tone was catatonic.
'Do you hate me?'
'... *you*... did that... to *me*?'
'Yes, yes, I told you, didn't I?' she replied, aggressive with guilt. 'So now you know. You see? It wasn't fate, after all.'

'I mean, you actually—'

She dived onto his shoulder again. Her head jerked up and down, whimpering. She lay in that position for some time. Only when she noticed that his body was convulsing too did she lift her head.

'Oh darling,' she said, looking up into his moist eyes, 'don't be up—'

But he wasn't upset. He was streaming tears of laughter.

It was the one reaction she hadn't anticipated.

'You actually had the courage to do it,' he explained, shaking his head.

'You mean you... don't mind?'

'Of course I mind!' he barked. 'It's disgraceful.' Then he went quiet again. 'I just... never thought you'd dare.' He pinched her cheek with his thumb and forefinger. 'Aren't you the most extraordinary woman?'

She didn't take her eyes off him. She wasn't yet sure whether this was genuine, whether his bright, smiling features weren't suddenly going to darken. He could be so devious. And he had pinched her too hard: her cheeks were stinging. But wasn't such violence natural in the circumstances, a kind of brash affection? She must be sure though. His expression—that was the clue. It wasn't simply bright; it was young again, young with fresh discovery.

The coast, she felt, was clear.

'You perverse thing,' she risked.

'Me? Well, I like that. You might have killed me.'

She shuddered. 'Don't even say it.' Then, after a moment: 'You could press charges. I'd understand.' He shook his head vehemently. 'I never thought you'd take it this way.'

'But you knew I was different,' he reminded her.

'Not *that* different.'

There was a pause. His expression became serious.

'You love me enough to...'

'You can see that then?'

He nodded. 'All the same, I am appalled. You're a prize bitch, Gillian.'

Her face fell for a moment.

'But I'm even more of a bastard,' he smiled reassuringly, 'so that's all right.'

They hugged each other passionately. It was a moment they felt they'd always remember. Alas the memory would be a mixed blessing; for just at that moment the old man pushed back his blankets, and pointed something in their direction.

Within days of leaving the hospital Mr Preston was to be seen tramping up and down the Charing Cross Road. As usual, he was laden with carrier bags. But his purpose was rather different this time. Instead of coming out with them, he was going in. Tentatively at first, and then with gathering speed, he was selling off his collection. Or the bulk of it. The shopkeepers bought the books back at an inferior rate. They were not pleased, however: some of the titles they had hoped never to see again.

A month after the completion of his task, and Mr Preston was back. As he came through the door, silence: you could hear a jaw drop. Then expectation. Ah! he had come to his senses again (or lost them); they washed their hands in anticipation of the familiar assault. But they were to be disappointed. He was there more to test himself than anything else. If he had wanted a book he would have had to suppress the urge; in the end, finding nothing that he needed, he had to *force* himself to buy one. As the days went by, he waited for the aftershocks. And waited. None were forthcoming. He went browsing intermittently at his leisure. He was cured.

At home Mrs Preston was busy dismantling shelves (thoroughly this time). The original ones, in the hall and living-room, were left standing. She cleaned up the nursery, furnished it with a bed, a rocking-horse, some cuddly toys. She must make it more habitable. He sat in the corner reading—reading her, that is: every now and then he would dampen down her zeal. He criticised her style: too many embellishments, he said. And, passive, she listened: he was right: she too must compromise.

Step by careful step then, without the fostering of too many illusions, they had decided to take on a child.

3

Collectors

It would not be true to say that all collectors are male. Women collect too, perhaps in more limited areas: books on cats, for instance, handicrafts, and more especially children's books—the illustrated kind (Dulac, Rackham, Nielsen), the girls' story books (Angela Brazil, Elinor Brent-Dyer), or moveables from Meggendorfer to modern pop-ups. In his book *With All Faults*, David Low cites Rose Macaulay as a famous example, and doubtless there have been many others. But male collecting tends to be more extreme; if it doesn't always drive their wives to thoughts of murder, it can take on the importance of another woman in the conflict of affections. There are people who dabble in collecting, who will only ask after a certain author if they happen to be passing a bookshop; but there are others who spend so much time there, so much money, it's as if they've moved in and are paying the weekly rent.

Why men more than women? I don't know if this gender difference has been satisfactorily explained, and I am at best a pretty mean psychologist—tough on people too—but let me venture a theory. I suspect that it has something to do with appetite (men tend to be greedier than women, both mentally and physically), with a primeval hunting instinct, and the competitiveness that goes with it. Because they have at the very least the potential to nurture a human life, women tend to be less selfish, to put more into their relationships, whether with children, parents, men or each other. If they have careers, they will expend a lot of energy in that direction too, and the practical application of this will probably be enough to satisfy their egos. This is not to say that careers and relationships aren't equally important to men, but as I say, they're greedy, they still have room to cultivate something else, and that thing is... well, themselves.

What they collect may well illuminate an aspect of their personality, but above all I think it represents what they would like *other people* to think of them. This kind of man is more into titivating his mental than his physical image, and I think his awareness of the impossibility of knowing everything, or even very much at all, makes him settle for a particular area he can manage and call his own. But he remains deeply insecure. In the same way that men have been known to compare the size of their equipment (I was thinking, actually, more on the hi-fi than on the Y-front), no doubt there are others who compare the size of their book collections. Indeed they may not even know their chosen subject; as I illustrated in my story, there are many who don't read what they collect. This is full-blown collectivitis. The book itself, the artefact, is merely the symbol of his knowledge; and like the other kind of cymbal it can make a big bang (Schopenhauer! Wittgenstein!), but sound him out on philosophy, and what you're likely to get is a proudly flourished quotation, and then... the rest is silence. Possession is all to him—knowledge at his fingertips, in the unlikely event he should ever require it.

This is one aspect of collecting; another is, of course, nostalgia. Peter Pan is not the only boy who would not grow up; a lot of men are attached to the past, whether in the shape of things they read as a child (Biggles, Billy Bunter), or places that exist no more (old topographical books), or buses and ships and choo-choo twains from a bygone era. If growing up is a process of compromise, disillusion and fast-accumulating responsibilities, then here is a convenient escape route to lost innocence, to an altogether slower, more leisurely world to which they can cling. Absolutely spiffing, what! This is where the book trade crisscrosses that of ephemera; indeed in one case I can think of, the two actually came together.

Tram-ticket Man! He used to haunt every shop, every book fair, up and down the country—wherever he was allowed, that is; he must have got banned from some places. He was a veritable valium in human form, a loiterer outside shop windows who would press his goggling eyes up to the glass, peering in to see which members of staff were present, and whether or not they would tolerate him. Scenting that the coast was clear, he would creep in, nod hesitantly, shuffle over to a shelf with an irksome air of mischief, and start poring over every book (pouring with sweat, too, he was so tense with anticipation). He worked systematically, from left to right, tentatively opening each one in such a way as to determine whether there was a wider gap than usual between the pages. Nothing. Blank after blank after blank. Just occasionally, his zombie-like features would light up with an alarming fanaticism, zing-zing-zing went his heartstrings, for behold! *there* was a tram ticket, but... no, his crest would fall, it was one he already had, circa 1926, stage 4 of the No.33 in Glasgow. He would put it back between the pages, close the book and return it to the shelf. And then the next book, and the next, worming his way through them until, after a while, losing faith in this particular shelf, he would try another, in a different room, and one could forget about him altogether.

For hours.

Just before closing he would eventually emerge, as if out of the woodwork, holding aloft perhaps one ticket for all his pains, in such a way as to say, 'I'm not just walking slyly off with this, but after all, it isn't a book, so there's no need for me to pay for it?', and shuffle off to his next port of call. I suppose with every collecting year his mission became harder, fewer and fewer previously undiscovered tram tickets would come into his possession, the eyes got soggier and baggier, the lethargy of the compulsive hoarder ground him to a halt. Until a few months would pass, six, a year, and one would suddenly remember one hadn't seen him for a long time. And the reason? Surprise, surprise. He'd shuffled off completely, bought the last ticket of all (and possibly the first), a one-way ticket to meet that great Collector in the sky.

And it was only then that we realised how much we missed him after all. What? Is that what you want me to say? Oh reader, you disappoint me, and I'm afraid you've stumbled into the wrong book. I've got your number all right: I suggest you pay a visit to Miss Hanff up the road at 84. Stick a 19 in front of that, and you'll have a better idea of what to expect on these premises.

I'm glad his collection didn't fall into my province: granted, a million tram tickets would not weigh as much as a hundred books, but going to the houses of such obsessives can be a nightmarish experience. I remember hearing of a house in a state of utter dilapidation, with peeling walls and threadbare carpets, with dry rot, mildew and rampant fungus, with dust so thick it actually dimmed the light, and then in the midst of it all, as if to redeem a life of shabby mismanagement, a vast collection of brown paper parcels. Uniform, square-shaped creatures, standing to attention on shelves, arranged in battle lines along the floor, patrolling the hallway and patrolling the stairs, invading every room from attic to cellar, a parcel seemingly for every square foot (and every foot *was* square), yes, a billeted army of books. On a closer inspection, these books were already in dust-jackets, and many of these jackets were carefully wrapped in cellophane, yet they still lived inside the paper bags in which they had been placed at the time of purchase; worse, some of these bags themselves were enclosed in a larger carrier bag, making (overall) four protective layers against decay. Of course, if he had only vacuumed his house occasionally, none of it would have been necessary. Instead there was this disparity between the out-and-out squalor to which he had consigned himself, and the books that survived him, fully intact, pristine.

The library, if I remember rightly, was all of literary criticism, and it has struck me since, why would anyone collect such works only, and not literature itself? Even if he were a critic or academic, such a man would surely have a stock of original texts as well. And this was in the days before elevation of that bugbear, literary theory, to its current place of eminence, i.e. before it became fashionable to regard literature as of secondary importance, and deconstruction of the text (the 'con' in the middle doesn't con me) as primary. Prejudiced... *moi*? Perhaps this collector had got through more than one collection (and more than one house); he'd already had a vast library of the classics, and now was onto a second, even drier (or dustier) than the first, just as some men have a second family. (And who knows, if he'd lived on, he might have started a third, a collection of critical works on critics, books about books about books. Once start along this road, and there is no limit to how far removed one can get from the original, from life itself.)

The breadth of collectors' interests varies considerably. I know of one gentleman who only buys editions of *The Natural History of Selborne*, a pioneering late-eighteenth-century study of the flora and fauna of a small Hampshire town, and precursor of all those works by Victorian amateur naturalists, reverends and the like, who set about exploring their own local areas. It is not as narrow as it sounds; the book went into hundreds of editions, in different formats, with different illustrations—it even merits its own bibliography, Edward A. Martin's of 1934. By the standards of some collectors, however, it is a little restricted. A literary equivalent might be the works of Emily Brontë (though try and find an early *Wuthering Heights*) or Alain-Fournier, who wrote only the one novel before being claimed by the First World War.

I suspect that some collectors deliberately choose the opposite, an author who may not even be their personal favourite but who has provided vast quantities of written matter to track down: H.G. Wells, P.G. Wodehouse, Somerset Maugham. But you'd be surprised how quickly even Maugham's scores and scores of titles can be snapped up. When a collector has all the first editions of an author, he will start upgrading these, trading off inferior copies against better ones; when he has achieved this, he will move onto the first American editions, the first colonial editions, the first 'cheap' editions, the first paperback editions (yes, I'm aware that I'm bludgeoning you with 'editions' but I'm trying to convey the relentlessness of it all), the first editions of other authors with an introduction by him, and so on and so forth, and fifth, each book in its many and varied manifestations, its appearances down the ages to different generations of readers. And if he gets bored with this, he can always start (and you try and stop him) collecting biographies of Maugham, critical studies on him, works that contain fleeting references to him, books autographed by him, editions of letters or indeed the letters themselves, original manuscripts. Still not satisfied? How about books by people who were close to Maugham, his wife Syrie, an authority on interior decoration, his nephew Robin, a novelist in his own right, author of *The Servant*. Of course, if things really got out of control, you could extend it further. Instead of stopping sensibly at the scarcely relevant *Servant*, you could lose it altogether, and by further association move onto the screenplay of the film that followed, written by one Harold Pinter (Mr Maugham, come in, Mr Maugham, we're not reading you now). And then you've done it, you've arrived on the funny farm, instead of taking the hint from this new author and allowing a significant pause, you've rushed ever onwards on your frantic quest, you're collecting firsts of *The Caretaker*, *The Birthday Party*, and you don't even remember why.

Goo-goo-ga-ga.

This is not as absurd as it sounds. People do move from one collection to another. More usually, they grow out of a particular interest, or become fed up with seeing the same books on their shelves every day. One man I knew had a large collection of monographs on British painters from Holbein to Bacon, then decided to shift into a more exotic gear, collecting books on Indian art instead. (Needless to say, to finance this, he had to sell off his hard-won first collection.) Goodness gracious me! Another reason for this change of heart might well be the neurosis that most collectors suffer from: it is not the fear that they will never round off their collection; it is, on the contrary, the fear that they *will*. Man is by nature an aspiring creature; indeed it was such curiosity that led to our 'first disobedience', it was for handling forbidden fruit that we were originally thrown out of Paradise. That long yearning reach still brings with it the promise of pleasure; plucked, and all that's left is the glut of consumption.

Collecting habits change, but only so much. Sometimes it is one of genre: there has recently been a huge upsurge in the price of cookery books, for instance—is this, too, nostalgia, in an age beset by the twin evils of junk food on the one hand, and obsessive dieting on the other? More often than not, there are changes *within* the genre. Modern first editions remain as popular as when I first entered the book trade, but as well as the usual collectable classics from the literary heights (Joyce etc.) to the commercial depths (Ian Fleming and the like), there has been more of a shift, I think, towards living authors. Conrad and Forester have always been sought after, and they still are, but there's as much interest in contemporary seafarers, especially Patrick O'Brian and Dudley Pope. Some current figures are popular in themselves (Terry Pratchett, Iain Banks), and others are made more so by a TV series (the Lovejoy novels of Jonathan Gash, Colin Dexter's Inspector Morse stories, Bernard Cornwell's Sharpe). Film also plays a significant role in boosting prices. A few years ago Thomas Keneally's *Schindler's Ark* was the sort of book that made you groan, turning up as it did every fortnight; one might have sold a first edition for £10. Since Spielberg turned it into a cinematic epic, the book has been in constant demand and—wouldn't you know it?—all but disappeared. It changes hands now for as much as £150! (Such is the influence of film indeed that the paperback is now entitled *Schindler's List*.) Then there is *The English Patient*: it, too, must have had a decent print run (the author had already written several books), it's only a few years old, and yet it recently peaked at £300 (now it's plummeting down again). Its literary merit is apparently of less importance than its success as a home-grown celluloid product stamped with Oscar approval.

This cynical trend seems likely to continue, so if you happen to hear that some previously unsaleable book is about to be turned into a multi-million dollar extravaganza, I advise you to start buying up all available copies. I think more and more people are going into collecting the way others speculate on the stock market; books as little as a few years old can start fetching phenomenal prices because of some publishing hype that sends a shock wave through the whole second-hand industry. As I write, *The Ice House*, the first book of the relatively new crime writer Minette Walters, published in 1993, is going for as much as £800, practically on a par with *Cover Her Face*, the first book of the long-established P.D. James, which dates from 1962. Why? Because people got it into their heads that on the basis of two or three thrillers she was this generation's foremost crime writer, and would go on being collectable in the longer term, thus stocking up on the first edition of her debut novel in anticipation of future demand. It's a hell of a risk. To buy them up at cover price, before the word is out, and the book has gone into a second impression, fine; but £800! No one can predict whether this bubble will burst in a short space of time (ker-splat! even before this book comes off the press) or whether she will indeed go on to consolidate her somewhat premature position. I suppose the market is being infiltrated by so many dealers and collectors and dealer-collectors that this kind of financial seesawing will become more and more prevalent.

All subjects, in whatever shape or form, are game for collectors. From nineteenth-century sets of the classics in beautiful morocco bindings to those ersatz leatherette travesties published by Heron; from books on the prehistory of cinema to the golden age of radio; *catalogue raisonnés* of Old Masters or, alternatively, complete sets of Giles cartoon annuals; masters of the macabre on the one hand, great humorists on the other; the leisurely pastimes of golf and cricket or the life-and-death struggles of military action; books on Louis XV furniture or books on buttons and biscuit tins. True crime, too, has a niche; but as I suspect it mostly attracts true criminals, I've let it lag somewhat behind (joke). I refuse to dabble in it; I mean, if they pay by credit card, how do you know it's theirs? The name might be Barrington Fortescue, but if the guy looks more like Lefty Magee...

Some people have a taste for the occult: astral projection, vampires, devil-worship, or even death itself. Oh yes, out there is a collector of books on suicide, grave-robbing, cemeteries—and what will it say on his epitaph?

RIP [initials] ASH (formerly of Gravesend)

'Life was but an ante-room, death was your study,
With the Grim Reaper you were on the best of terms;

Well congratulations! you've graduated (morbid bloody
Old sow-and-sow). And hats off to the worms.'

But not all collectors are so narrow; nor is subject-matter the only guiding principle. There are those who just love finely made books, and might have something in every field I have just listed; and those who are not really collectors at all, but omnivorous readers for whom the content of the book is more important than the object itself, resulting in a library more notable for its promiscuity than fidelity to a single idea. Another perennial is the small-is-beautiful or pocketability factor: the King Penguin series published just after the war; the Collins, Everyman or Oxford classics; or, diminishing in size still further, miniature books, coming in at less than two inches tall. Naturally this extends to paperbacks. There are myriad collectors of the first 500 Penguins (from No.1, *Ariel*, onwards), or others of a certain date, like the olive-green ones of the seventies. Some prefer the trashier productions of the fifties (Ace, Four Square, Corgi), with their sensational covers of *femmes fatales* and dope fiends. Most valuable of all are publishers' proof copies, books-to-be in their final stage of preparation; because they pre-date the first editions in hardback form, these rather flimsy, drab, perfunctory paperbacks are often worth even more. Clearly they have a historic importance, but they are hardly decorative.

Others collect books for a certain kind of binding, whether vellum, pigskin or 'papier mâché'; or for their dust-jacket design (John Minton, Brian Cook, E. McKnight Kauffer); or because they have a fore-edge painting (a sketch, usually of a landscape, that only springs to life if you concertina the pages at a certain angle—most of these are fake, i.e. painted in at a later date). I am sure, if one went to see enough private libraries, one would discover countless other common denominators: people who collect books that are green, for instance, or published in the year of their birth, even with their name concealed in the title.

Indeed the word 'title' recalls to mind another collector who asked me round to his Chelsea flat to do a valuation. I didn't really need the statuette of Michelangelo's *David* or the colour scheme of a rather bilious shade of pink to help orient myself, as it were, in this gentleman's somewhat louche apartment. Nor was it the fact that as I went through his books I discovered author after author of a particular bent (Gide, Genet, Virginia Woolf). No, his distinctive style was to collect everything that fitted in (however superficially) with his theme. For every modern classic from *The Well of Loneliness* to *The Swimming Pool Library*, for every Cecil Beaton or Rex Whistler dust-jacket, there was a thoroughly heterosexual item that got compromised by virtue of the company it kept: Bret Harte's *The Luck of the Roaring Camp*, for instance, Chesterton's *Club of Queer Trades*, or Andrew Lang's 'fairy' books. Auden and Swinburne one might expect but between them stood, or rather languished, *The Poetical Works of John Gay*; a book on Lesbos naturally, but Offa's Dyke, surely not; *Inversion, Sexual Deviance*, and then bringing up the rear, so to speak, a sober history of *Cottage Industries*.

Books I had never considered of even innuendo potential were forever divested of their innocence: *Men Without Women, Three Men in a Boat, Seven Men and Two Others*. *Now* they seem obvious victims, but before... The catalogue was relentless: *Pacific Rim, Dangling Man*, a biography of Tyrone Power by Hector Arce (*sic*—it gets considerably sicker). One title puzzled me: *Háry János*, a book on the Kodály orchestral suite—or it did until my host got his tongue round it, at which point all was revealed in graphic detail. It didn't even stop at titles. I flicked through a few books to ensure they were in good condition internally, and found... annotations. The introduction to Wilfred Owen's *Collected Poems* referred to his *annus mirabilis*, but of course Mr Pink had crossed out one of the letters.

I like to think I am not especially homophobic (any metropolitan bookseller will tell you that a large proportion of serious readers are gay), indeed I'm convinced that many homosexuals (especially in loving relationships) are rather more civilised than their straight counterparts. Still I have to admit to a certain nervousness when I left his establishment. I was ushered into the narrowest lift I have ever seen, closely followed by Mr Pink himself, standing only inches away from me, and confronting me with *the* most beamingly suggestive smile on his face. It was not that I feared he would try anything, but that his smile was so infectious that I could feel the corners of my mouth twitching, and an answering smile, in such a constricted environment, could be misinterpreted. Luckily I remained serious, no, positively severe, throughout our brief descent, and when we came out onto the porch, shook hands with him rather more firmly than usual. I was about to hail a cab when he offered to drop me off himself—he had an appointment in the West End, he said. I declined his offer: it was late, my working day was finished, I lived near enough to walk home. But that's not what I said... oh no. What on earth induced me to get my words so Freudianly twisted at this late stage?

'That's very kind of you,' I remarked, 'but I'm going home straight.'

Talk about a bilious pink!

Without batting an eye, his reply was immediate. 'Of course you are, dear boy,' he licked his lubricious lips, 'and you have me to thank for that.'

4

Catalogues

One way for a collector to acquire the more elusive titles for his library is to put his name on a mailing list and order through booksellers' catalogues. This will save time certainly, time otherwise spent ferreting around in bookshops. It is unlikely to save money. For the point of a catalogue—at least a good one—is to be (let's not beat about the bush) expensive. Not all booksellers issue them; some don't have the need, and some, quite frankly, don't have the books. For those who do, however, the main advantage is what they can charge. But surely there would be no difference if the book just sat on the shelf for all to see? Wrong. If it just sat there, side by side with cheaper items, you would pick it up, turn in all innocence to the price on the first blank page, gasp with audible horror, and possibly abuse the man behind the desk.

But a book in a catalogue—at least at the time of issue—is not on the shelf, it is in the bookseller's inner sanctum, or even at his private address (many cataloguers work from home). Moreover when you're sitting at the breakfast table reading through his list he is out of earshot; your gasp (spluttering tea all over it) cannot be heard. Nor are you blinking at just one expensive item, but one among many; belonging to a select élite, it loses its individual power to offend. The ideal catalogue is a collection of choice books of a certain specialisation put together by someone with long experience and excellent taste. Far from being picked at random, they are known to be desirable, hard to find. And they have not been savagely handled; the public can't get its grubby little mitts on them. The price is fixed, all the more so as it is the first thing to be seen; you know what you have to pay before you even get to see the book. Some dealers and collectors will call up to reserve the ones they want, then come and view them; others will pay on the nail, without a single once-over, trusting to the accuracy of the description. A few will haggle, but the overall extent of this will be less than with the general public. Catalogues are designed to be exclusive, and the main thing to be excluded is the category called Ordinary People. (They will be dealt with, in no uncertain fashion, in a later chapter.)

But I have not yet come to the main reason why books in catalogues are expensive. It isn't merely that they are hand-picked, unseen, out of harm's way, and visibly price-tagged in advance of criticism. A catalogue is more than just a list of titles followed by long rows of figures; each item is *described*. Some books, we know, are born great, but others have greatness thrust upon them—in the form of shameless hyperbole. It is vital for the cataloguer to convey the preciousness of the object under discussion, even, to fetishise it, for his fervour may awaken a latent eroticism within the reader. For instance, he will invite you to savour the delights of an

> 'only known copy, in immaculate condition, exclusively bound up for the author by Sangorski Sutcliffe in maroon levant morocco, raised bands, spine decorated with printer's curlicue device, front cover inlaid with central panel embossed in gold with author's own initials, ornately tooled borders, all edges gilt, crêpe de Chine endpapers, on Van Gelder Holland wove paper, in specially prepared crushed velvet box, presentation copy of the author to himself with typically tongue-in-cheek (?) dedication on the title page: "To O.J.M. Davis with my everlasting love and respect".'

This is, of course, an extreme example, a book so rare it doesn't even exist (though come to think of it...). But you get the idea. And it's not just a question of luxurious imagery; there are sundry other ways of tweaking the purse-strings of the confirmed bibliophile:

'*Flush: a Biography*, 1st edition, 1933, Virginia Woolf's whimsical tale of Mrs Browning's dog, but not so whimsical as the printer, who here has printed "Woof" instead of Woolf, making this (as far as we know) a unique copy'

'1st edition, the most difficult in this series, 1,990 copies of the original 2,000 believed to have been destroyed in "a freak warehouse explosion" (this was the official line—others suspect the author himself took to deliberate arson, thus guaranteeing the book's rarity, and the rocketing value of the ten surviving copies, in his own possession naturally)'

'the book that may have cost the writer his life, and indeed signed by him on the title page, with the additional message, "written with my very heart's blood", a literal description we think, for we have forensically tested the shaky red scrawl'

'1st edition (1611 of course), Authorised Version of the Bible, "authorised" indeed, for it is signed by God on the front free endpaper to Shakespeare, an unusually late inscription this, with special note underneath:
"N.B. Remember when you write your next masterpiece, Billy-boy, just Who created your talent. And in case you don't believe Me, you're about to conceive your last play—for your revels now are ended—a nifty little number called *The Tempest*.
P.S. Don't you dare nick that phrase!"'

I exaggerate: very well then, I exaggerate: but then, so do catalogues. No publisher ever puffed out a blurb on the inner flap of a dust-jacket with more outrageous claims than a dealer does within the hushed, exalted confines of his plush little brochure. Some are guiltless, of course; they don't need to over-dramatise their wares because any punter worth his mettle will be aware of the scarcity of the book in question. But beware the long spiel, the piling on of adjective upon adjective: methinks the writer doth profess too much. It would doubtless be interesting to see, in a given year, all the catalogues issued by booksellers up and down the country, and determine just how usually a rare book turns up 'in unusually fine condition'.

So what makes a book desirable? Is it age, condition, rarity? To explain all this would probably take as long as I've been in the book trade (i.e. too long), and I'm still learning. But here are a few pointers. The most important thing to understand is the law of supply and demand. With modern first editions, for example, certain authors are widely collected, others are not (and it would take another book to explain why *this* is). Some are always in fashion, some are distinctly outmoded, and others veer between the two. P.G. Wodehouse, for instance, is a staple of the first-edition market; his quintessentially English world of daft upper-class people with more money than sense appeals to a high percentage of the population, let alone those rich (and by no means daft) enough to start collecting his works. For a bookseller it doesn't matter why; it is just *so*. On the other hand, the once-popular John Galsworthy has lost his niche. He still has a modest appeal for the American market, but his novels were apparently published in vast quantities, there are more copies floating around than customers to buy them. The third category is harder to pin down, but it seems to me that Doris Lessing, though still read by many, and still collectable, causes less of a ripple of excitement than she did perhaps ten years ago. Interest may well be restored, dare I say it, on her demise—such is the nature of literary necrophilia.

This is not to say that common books, like Galsworthy's, are necessarily cheap. The first (trade) edition of *Seven Pillars of Wisdom* by T.E. Lawrence turns up with regularity, but people always want it, such is the mystique surrounding this controversial figure. The same goes for Churchill's *Second World War* in six volumes or *History of the English-Speaking Peoples* in four—*very* common, but good sets can fetch £60–100, though if you based the price on how often you see them ... But yes, many books one sees all the time are inexpensive; because the market is saturated with them, they're not much sought after, or rather, because they're no longer treasured, people discard their copies, and the market is ... And so it goes round in circles.

Approaching from the opposite angle, rare books, those one hardly ever sees, are not necessarily valuable. Think of an author who can't get published, but who is so determined to get into print, and so bitter towards those who rejected him, that he finally resorts to paying for his own publication, perhaps in a limited edition of 500 copies. Vanity publishing. This book—let's call it *The Snigger of the Narcissus*—is not likely to turn up very often (and thank the Lord for it, judging by examples I've seen). But even if it did, it would be unlikely to sell, the chances being that the publishers turned it down for a very good reason. It might be signed, annotated by the author, bookmarked with various letters from him, and still no one would buy it (except perhaps the author himself, a friend or relation, or someone new to the game of buying and selling for profit, who might think that *every* signature...).

But if you combine the rarity factor with desirability (let's go back to Wodehouse, how about his first book, *The Pothunters*), then you have lift-off. Name your price. Do I hear £2,000? Probably more. Further, if you add to rarity and desirability the additional factor of fine condition, you're in orbit. Condition, they say, is all, and if you're talking about desirable books it is (again, I repeat, a mint copy of our *Snigger* is as worthless as a duff one). With literature, dust-jackets are all-important. A rare first edition, just the book, without its original wrapper, might be worth £200; but add a rough-looking dust-jacket and you might be doubling the price; add a dust-jacket complete, without tears, Sellotape marks, price-clipping, or even dust, and it could be three times more again.

A book might even have a normal ceiling price agreed by specialists who've only ever seen it in such-and-such condition; but if it should turn up in a state never seen before, I'm afraid that ceiling has to be raised. Have it signed by an author living and you're building a spiral staircase between the two floors of your new maisonette; an author dead, and you're using wrought iron; an ex-author who rarely signed anything, and you've gone clean through the second roof; a rare signature from one rotting author to another, and you can buy the flat above *this* one; combine all these with a long written comment, the sky's the limit. And so it goes on, with each new plus a multiplication of desirability.

Next, you need to know that the same book in identical condition can fetch more than another copy. Why? Well, look closely enough, and you'll find out that it isn't actually the same—but you'll need exceptional eyes, for it's often the difference of a single letter in a single word. Books often have issue points: that is, at the time of printing, as the sheets are bound up into cloth bindings, the first copies will come off the press, and perhaps a mistake will be spotted (and then corrected) before the other copies are ready. The result: the misspelling 'pedentic' on page 29 can make all the difference in future catalogues between a first issue price of £1,000 and a second issue (still the first *edition*, mind) of £500, with, don't forget, the corrected version of 'pedantic' instead. (Ironic, isn't it, that it's the one with the mistake that's more desirable.) Stumbling onto a first of this imaginary book, a person who really knows his stuff will turn immediately to page 29 and shout out an ecstatic '*Yes*' (baffling to fellow browsers) when he discovers the rarer misprinted version.

Lucky bugler![1]

First editions are a good thing to collect because, though there is the danger that your chosen author may become unfashionable, mere reprints make no difference (not so, for instance, with important reference works). It is the historic moment of birth, of impact, that attracts the aficionado. I stress again that the nearer it is in condition to how it was when first issued is the best gauge of its value. The book can be marred as much as the all-important dust-jacket: it can have pen underlining; be upside down, mispaginated or bleached by the sun; have the wrong binding (i.e. a library or remainder binding, not the original publisher's cloth); or an endpaper or title page

---

[1] Does your copy read 'bugler'? Congratulations.

ripped out. It will be obvious to those in the know, but a blank page is almost as important as a page of text, and the lack of one will seriously devalue any but the rarest books.

I have talked mostly of modern firsts, but there are, of course, catalogues on every subject. So what other contributory factors are there to a book's expensiveness? For one thing, historical importance (early editions in the history of science, philosophy, theology, political theory etc.); for another, the presence of plates (hand-coloured prints, steel and copper engravings, chromolithographs) in works of natural history and topography, cut out and framed by print dealers; or books out of a famous person's library. Most leather-bound or antiquarian tomes are of a certain commercial value, if only because they are relics from a bygone era, and then there is the sheer cost of the binding itself. Private press books, limited editions. But with twentieth-century books of a non-fictional nature, one is on very shaky ground.

It is impossible to generalise about modern productions, but one can be guided by a single golden rule: specificity. While there are no guarantees, it is true to say that a general book is less likely to be of value than one which probes a particular area and does so with consummate scholarship. For instance, a large encyclopaedia with a title like *Costumes of the World* may well be less valuable than a smaller-format but highly specific title such as *Costume in France in the Eighteenth Century*, especially if the latter looks detailed and is by a known authority on the subject (a curator of a museum perhaps, with other books under his belt). It will come as no surprise to you that there are well-researched, far from woolly large-format books (Max Tilke's is a classic reference work) and bad books of a narrow focus that trivialise their subject. Rules are made to be broken, and don't come running to me if you spend a hard-earned £10 on something that seems to fit my thesis, and then fail to sell it for more than a fiver. I tell you now in advance: *I won't refund you.*

Experience is all: you develop a nose for the definitive study in a particular area, you get to know names, sometimes the clue may even be in the blurb—no, it doesn't always lie—something like 'this is the most comprehensive study yet undertaken'; or in the extensive bibliography at the end; or the level of care lavished on the book's production (a silkier feel than usual to the cloth); or even the price (12 guineas for a book normally 6—though this could merely be a coffee-table book designed to sell exclusively to the toffs of the day). Use your own judgment: sometimes specificity is actually a drawback: well, imagine a book called *Hat-Making in Upper Volta in 1920*, as far as I know a bogus title, very specific certainly, in fact excessively so. Though there is undeniable interest in millinery, and a dearth of good books on the subject, only a handful of people will be *so* fascinated that they will have to acquire a copy. It is too obscure a subject for your common-or-garden milliner. Far more likely it will appeal to our good old friend the collector, or the kind called a 'completist', someone who must have every book on his (and in this case probably her) chosen subject. No, this is a case where a general guide to hats should sell far more quickly. Should. Books can be a little like racehorses; some that you would expect to set the pace are actually the slowest in the running; and others like *Hat-Making in Upper Volta in 1920* are real winners, romping home at 33–1. I'm afraid that someone out there is just going to have to write this book now, if only to prove me wrong. Worse, they may already have done so, and are preparing a libel suit as I speak.

I have talked a lot in this chapter about the hype of certain expensive catalogues: the frequency of the word 'rare', the commonness of 'scarce', the downright ubiquity of 'uncommon'. Granted, such terms tend to be abused, but at least these dealers are *trying*. How much more preferable is a catalogue of (at the very least) not-so-usual books at fancifully inflated prices, to only-too-familiar items which proliferate in the catalogues of countless amateur booksellers. Really, if they can't do any better than an average of £10 or £20 per book, can't whet the appetite with exorbitant words and/or prices, with 'inner *dentelles*', 'rococo embellishments' and 'almond *doublures*', they shouldn't be compiling catalogues at all. Clearly they can have no idea how dull their compilations are, or they would never dare to waste printers' time and their own money in producing these assaults on the good taste of Mr Bibliophile. They ought to be more honest with themselves.

Now being an extremely honest person myself, one who would never describe a book in more flattering terms than it deserves, I would like to round off this chapter with a catalogue of my own. So far I have covered the nonexistent, the unusual and the thoroughly mediocre—but that still leaves plenty of leeway. Now what I am about to compile is a list of some of the greatest dogs in my profession, howlers you might call them, barking their way into (and rarely out of) every bookshop up and down the country. If I can't in such a short space direct you to those books you ought to buy (to ensure an early retirement), I can tell you which you ought definitely to avoid (to avert bankruptcy). These are not necessarily bad books (in this respect the second-hand book trade is decidedly unfair), often quite the contrary; but they are now forgotten, or unwanted, at any rate they turn up all the time. You have been warned.

I should begin, as all cataloguers do, by telling you your rights:

(a) Unless otherwise stated, all books are first English editions (and no more valuable for that), in original cloth, and were published in London (that they were published anywhere is, to a regular frequenter of bookshops, unfortunate). Books are in dust-wrappers only when stated (i.e. always—it's Sod's Law that the duffest titles appear in the finest condition!).

(b) When it comes to the titles in *this* catalogue, single copies only are rare. Generally speaking, I have multiples, desperate for a home, and though I have to cover myself and say they're subject to availability, you can take it from me they'll be around for yonks. I accept all forms of payment (credit cards, postal orders, cheques, cash, booze, ciggies, anything).

(c) Every effort has been made to describe these books accurately. Any title found not to be up to scratch (or even considerably better) would surprise me, but whatever happens please do not return the book, as

your refusal will seriously offend. It goes without saying I'll happily reimburse you; I just don't want the book back under any circumstances.
(d) Books will be dispatched abroad (and good riddance) at the earliest opportunity, and if I can't find a carrier (the *fuss* people make about rabies) I'll deliver them myself—even to Upper Volta. I can safely say that postage, packing and insurance (you mean you really want these books insured?) are absolutely free—after all, you're doing me a favour.
(e) All prices in this catalogue are net (yeah yeah, blah-di-blah), but between you and me I'm extremely flexible, in fact I'm a real pushover, even those of you who are really bad at haggling can probably twist my arm.
Please send all correspondence to: O.J.M. Davis, The Kennels, North Labrador, Barkshire
Website: gr.owl. bow.ow.ow/chi-hua-hua.
My opening hours are Sunday–Sunday 6am–6am. Please call whenever you feel like it, even in the middle of the night, I can't sleep you see, they're always pining, pining for a home, you've no idea what it means to be shot of these mangy beasts, I could tell you stories, but... hell... just surf me, why don't you?...

CATALOGUE 1

(and only—I suspect these books will be available for ages, so what need to compile another?)
I have dispensed with alphabetical order; it's more convenient for me to list these books in ascending order of commonness:

 (1) THE HISTORY OF THE ROD:
   WILLIAM COOPER   £10

Actually not all that common (I've only had sixteen of these in the last five years), but I couldn't resist saying that

I have a fine, spanking copy, a must for any masochist (i.e. collectors of highly unsought-after material).

(2) THE SINGER NOT THE SONG:
AUDREY ERSKINE LINDOP £5

A frequent visitor (and one that tends to outstay its welcome), good copy as always in fine d/w, a novel about some Mexican bandit and his involvement with a priest. As interesting as it sounds. And yours for next to nothing (a song indeed).

(3) THE CRASH OF '79: PAUL ERDMAN £2

Oh dear, we're getting very common now, this one's a right little scrubber, turns up in most charity shops, usually (as here) with d/w, a book for every student of business in that memorable year 1979, the end of a 'low dishonest decade' (or was that the thirties?).

(4) THE WATERS UNDER THE EARTH:
JOHN MOORE £1

Quite frankly, the best place for it.

(5) THE EGG AND I: BETTY MACDONALD 50p

Love that title, it stays in the mind, doesn't it, it stays in one's field of vision too, whether large, small or regular (yoke), indeed I have three copies of *The Egg and I*, say it often enough and it sounds like 'agony'.

(6) THE AGONY AND THE ECSTASY:
IRVING STONE FREE

Plenty of the former certainly, but only you can supply the latter, no, I don't mean in tablet form, just relieve me of a copy. It's about Michelangelo and the Sistine Chapel, you see, I know it intimately, I've read pages of it, well, page one several times (much the same thing), that's as far as I could get.

CATALOGUES

(7) SHAKESPEARE: IVOR BROWN −£5

Ivor fiver for anyone who will take this old warhorse off my hands. I'm not proud, I've got 22 copies, pristine in d/w (OK, two are slightly foxed, you get a tenner for those), do take one, I mean every book comes into the world with the same rights as any other, it's entitled to a home, a family, contact with other books, who knows but with a bit of affection old Ivor might stop barking. Down, boy!

(8) THE POETICAL WORKS OF
ROBERT BRIDGES −£10

So he was once Poet Laureate, no one ever thought he was that good, and to add insult to injury, not only do I have 28 hardbacks in excellent condition, some bastard publisher went and did a paperback recently. When I think of all the deleted titles, and they go and reprint that, I tell you it's enough to make me start barking.

(9) LIKE WATER, LIKE FIRE: AN ANTHOLOGY
OF BYELORUSSIAN VERSE −£20

Grrrrrr! Stop that, this isn't Browning you know, I can't hear myself think! Like it or not, I've got 35 copies of this unique collection, buy the lot and you've earned £700, surely some enterprising schoolteacher (come on, you're always short of money) can place this on his syllabus, look, if you don't buy these doggerel verses no one else will, I just haven't... got... the room any more.

(10) THE BIG SLEEP: RAYMOND CHANDLER ?

Caught you! You really were napping, weren't you? The monumental dullness, the veritable *Dunciad* of the above sent you off into an irresistible stupor, didn't it, now you've perked up a bit, thought I'd sell you a *Big Sleep*, no, pay you to take it away. Tough! It's a con, OK, I don't really have one, if I did do you think I'd still be here talking to... If, however, by any chance, you've got one, perhaps you'd, er, like to give

CATALOGUES

me a ring, I'm sure we could arrange something, you could have, say, all nine titles above (and with umpteen duplicates that's a lot of awful, I mean an awful lot of books). What do you say: the whole lot in exchange! Think about it. I certainly will—in fact, that's all I ever think about.[2]

---

[2] We apologise to our readers, but at the time of going to press we had no idea how mentally unstable Mr Davis had become: he is now residing at an exclusive private address. Customers who wish to purchase any of the above-mentioned titles are advised to join Mr Davis immediately... sorry, that was uncalled for, these customers are now directed to all bad bookshops, where, we feel certain, you can pick up a copy any time.

5

Browsing in Bookshops

There are many collectors, however, who never buy from catalogues. To have the work cut out for them, to have a book more or less handed over to them on a plate, is to drain the pleasure out of what should be the slow, patient, cumulative process of building a library. For some, money is not a problem but they might still prefer to be economical; for others, money is distinctly a problem, they are constantly behind in their credit card payments, or barely able to pay the mortgage. But can bargains still be found in bookshops? Sometimes it seems impossible to find anything seriously under-priced, everyone appears to know exactly what they're doing, and then... bang! there it is. It's often a book so obviously desirable I barely bother to open it to check the price (by the law of averages, I must have missed a few this way). How many dealers before me, I speculate, have stopped before this book, fallen victim to their greedy curiosity, opened it, had their suspicions confirmed, and put it back with a slight grumble? No, I won't be the umpteenth one to repeat this Pavlovian procedure; I'm cleverer than that, not so predictable. Foolish, in fact. For it can be worthwhile: you can't be sure that other dealers have looked at it, you don't know when this particular book arrived on this particular shelf (unless you check that shop every day!). You have to be in the right place at the right time. Best of all would be to turn up as an item is being purchased over the counter, linger nonchalantly in the background while it is being priced (though mentally crouching on all fours), and then pounce before the owner even places it on the shelf.

BROWSING IN BOOKSHOPS

'Excuse me, can I have a look at that?'
'Why, it's only just come in.'
'Is that right? And how much is it?'
'Ten pounds, sir.'
'There you go. Thanks. And goodbye.'
'Heh... don't you want a receipt?'

No, I do not, it's cash slap down in his palm and I'm out of there, before anyone else, dealer, collector or significant other, can get his hands on it. For a good book at a low price is winged like Mercury, it won't last long on a shelf; often it's a matter of minutes, maybe hours, seldom days. (A bad book never even reaches fledgling status, remains stuck there with superglue.) But I should make one thing clear. I'm not one of those dealers who go round shouting from the rooftops about what great finds they've had—I have a fear of heights for one thing, and that's metaphorical as well as literal: I'm strictly small-time and prefer it that way. I've had some modest successes, the occasional gift, and I've also wasted a great deal of precious time getting nowhere. For some bookshops are not only as expensive as catalogues, but more so.

I suspect there are many reasons for this. One, of course, is ignorance: they simply don't know what they're doing, perhaps they've never even seen a decent book before, so as soon as one swims into their ken, they get over-excited. Another is defiance: if lazy cataloguers can get away with it, take just ten seconds to type a few numbers into their word processors and then it's £500 thank you very much, then so can they, with brass bloody knobs on, especially with their overheads. A third is an amalgam of patience and ambition, with just a smattering of greed: who's to say that if the going price of a book is £100, one can't get £120 if one waits a while (and it may be several years, by which time inflation will have done its bit and the book really is worth £120!). Such a way of thinking could, if combined with quiet confidence, sound buying technique and above all a good location, result in someone becoming a market leader; equally, if combined with cockiness, careless risk-taking, and some God-forsaken cul-de-sac for premises, it could lead to financial ruin.

There is still a myth going round that provincial booksellers are cheaper than metropolitan ones. This myth, I suspect, is perpetuated by people who *potter about* in bookshops (i.e. not dealers or serious collectors). I'm sure that if you do this, and have a taste for certain cheap dull books at the bottom end of the market, you may find what you would consider a bargain in these fabled backwaters. And that's about it. I'm not old enough to talk with authority about the past, but I think in the days before book fairs came in—where scores of booksellers congregate at a select venue in a provincial town, offering their wares ostensibly to the public though actually more to each other—before they learned through such mutual contact the going price of a book, yes, inevitably, there must have been bargains to be had. Obviously a dealer in the heart of a city doing business with hundreds of people every day would have known more about market forces than an old biddy next to 'ye olde tea shoppe', whose idea of a good day was selling three moth-eaten paperbacks. But nowadays, if it's an established business, they're likely to know what they're doing, whether in country town or city. They may deliberately 'price for the trade', charge, say, £15 for a £30 book, because they have lots of stock and prefer a fast turnover; but a real bargain is exceptional, not the rule.

Unless perhaps you're lucky enough to stumble onto a new business starting up in the middle of nowhere, property of a retired couple who've spent their working lives doing other things but have always fancied their own little bookshop in some quiet nook for their declining years. Lambs to the slaughter! I once got chatting to such a woman from Bradford-on-Avon. She was enthusing away to me about her love of books and how she and her husband were just about to open this shop, they'd inherited a library, of course they couldn't claim to know *everything* yet, in fact they were fairly new to the game, she meant, some books were worth as much as £50 weren't they, but she was sure they'd learn in time, it was all a matter of experience wasn't it, and if I was passing that way it might be worth—

'And where exactly?' I interrupted this garrulous creature, my nostrils already beginning to flare, my pupils dilate.

Between bouts of further (unsolicited) autobiography, I did just manage to pin down an address. Unfortunately I was very busy just then, I couldn't get away for a few days, but oddly enough, I found myself lining up the following weekend for an off-the-cuff visit to... yes, Bradford-on-Avon, the heart of Wiltshire, England's green and pleasant land etc., etc. My arcadian fantasy was just beginning to take wing when, two days later, the woman called, practically in tears, to inform me that she'd been cleaned out completely. All her best books had gone, even some of her worst (she meant, did people still read *Ulysses*, it was all Greek to her, Shakespeare and Company indeed), some blasted dealer had got there before me. Presumably she'd made some money, but that wasn't the point, her dream of some late-flowering day-to-day hobby was shattered. So was I. If someone had to ruin her life, I thought, why couldn't it have been me? No no, that's unkind of me—and *to* me, if it comes to that; if I didn't know me so well I'd sue, at the very least meet me outside in ten minutes. Actually it was very decent of her to ring; otherwise I might have made an utterly fruitless journey. (I never did like the countryside anyway; five minutes without pavement and I start to panic.)

I am generalising now, but I've come to the conclusion that when it comes to bookshops in country towns there are three main types: the cheap, the posh and the interesting. Quite often a town will have all three. By 'cheap' I don't mean you can make a killing there; no, I mean the books are crap, cheap maybe, but crap. They stock recent children's annuals, hordes of sci-fi and horror paperbacks, branch railway books, interminable British topography, esoterica and sport, and let's not forget those wretched how-to-do-it art books which only serve to encourage yet another generation of arthritic watercolourists. Dullsville—distinctly for those who *potter about*. Yes, you've guessed it, I hate that phrase: in my experience, it is used either by those who lead sorry, purposeless existences, or those who, on the contrary, dash off a novel in the morning, a string quartet in the afternoon, but on being asked what they've been doing, always reply: 'oh nothing much—just pottering about'.

Now the second class of bookshop, the 'posh', is at the other extreme. They may well have ordinary books, even a few bad ones, but their general stock is of a high quality, they have a large antiquarian section, rare editions, scholarly books, and all at very correct, actually seldom over-the-top prices. It's all rather forbidding and austere, but there's never anything improper, like an extra nought where you least expect it. These shops cater for rich country folk, nowadays mostly retired people, City types who have a rural retreat and want to line their walls with leather, or other dealers who have a customer for a particular rarity. There's usually someone at the desk occupied in cleaning a binding with beeswax, collating a book with tipped-in plates, or working on the latest £50,000 catalogue. He looks up at you over his specs, takes you in at a glance to ensure you're not a thief, then goes back to his work. All very impressive, rather like walking into a library, at worst a morgue, and for me about as much chance of buying something. Not always. Some of the more general books can be cheaper than usual, as if he can't be bothered to price everything with scrupulous accuracy, indeed he probably sneers at items below £20.

Then there's the third class of bookshop—the 'interesting'. This is more my terrain. After a preliminary sniff I get the lie of the land, I sense distinct possibilities, there is an air of the topsy-turvy, the erratic. This class of bookshop varies considerably, but in quality terms it is pitched well above the plebeian and considerably below the aristocratic. Bad books may well preponderate, but no section is exclusively so, good stuff is mixed in, the owner is clearly trying to keep up a certain standard, he's not just a greengrocer who happens to sell books. The prices in such set-ups are more haywire than in their posh counterparts, but if some books are overvalued, just as many allow some room for manoeuvre. Such a shop is normally only as good as its last major buy: from an auction, or house clearance, or whatever. You can be lucky in your timing, grab some recent acquisitions, or you can be unlucky, in which case there's been nothing new for weeks. Or—yet again—you've been preceded by that scourge of our planet, the Other Dealer.

Think of Brighton, a seaside town fast becoming a shopper's paradise, crammed to bursting with bookshops, junk shops, antique arcades, more opportunity for browsing than any other provincial town in England (with the exception of Hay-on-Wye). Well, I once spent a whole day there, always just one step behind a dealer I knew. I went into the first shop and there he was, piling the boxes into his car, and—surprise, surprise—I could find nothing of interest in what remained. Then I moved onto the next one, and there he was again, already writing out a cheque, barely able to stop himself from smiling, a smugness which increased when he caught sight of me moving about, frowning, empty-handed. A third was the same—well, I didn't even bother to check this one out, I decided I had to get ahead of him, it got to the point where I deliberately changed direction, tried another place in an out-of-the-way part of town. Aha! no sign of him, at last I'd shaken him off. But there was nothing to buy. Maybe there never had been, far more likely, however, he'd done his vacuuming earlier. Bastard! Whenever I plan to visit Brighton now, I feel like ringing him up, just to ensure we don't synchronise our journeys once more. Doubtless I'd get his answering machine (have you noticed how it's more or less impossible to talk to anyone nowadays?):

> 'I'm sorry I'm not here to take your call. Please leave a message after the tone. And if it's O.J.M. Davis—it is you, isn't it?—all I can say is, don't even think about it. You know what I mean, don't you? If I'm not here, I must be somewhere else. Yes, even as I speak to you now, I'm cleaning up the whole of the south coast. Ever so sorry.
>
> 'This is Barry the bibliovore signing out.'

And he does so with an array of nasty nibbling noises.

But even if you don't find anything, going round bookshops can be an experience in itself. A constant fascination is the different methods employed by the staff in dealing with the public. The bespectacled owner of the posh emporium above chose to ignore me and let me get on with my browsing. But some people don't want to be ignored: they walk out. They're probably not regulars, they just require something for today and need help in finding it. Conversely, there are booksellers who refuse to acknowledge the concept of browsing, there must be some area that interests you, more than that, a particular book you've come in for, and they'll be damned if they can't get it out of you. I'm reminded of an even more extreme case, an acquaintance of mine who was actually *locked in*, held captive by a desperate tradesman, and only allowed to leave after he had purchased something. This was in a foreign country by the way, where else but America—they do things differently there.

I think there has to be a mean between aloofness and belligerence; you must look up and assess every customer in his or her own right, they will usually make it clear by their eye contact (or lack of it) whether they want your assistance or not. Some just want a little guidance, especially if there isn't a shop plan, and then to be left alone; others want you to tell them if you have a book in stock, to put your finger on it if you have, and to look for it even when you *know* you haven't. These people have so often been disappointed that they've turned into boa constrictors: they'll squeeze you dry for every last scrap of information, sometimes it seems they'll never let you go (the consumer equivalent of our tradesman above).

Indeed the relationship between a bookseller and his customers is not quite like any other; complex power games are at work, curious nuances of domination and submission. The bookseller has the right of way in that he owns the premises, and yet... 'the customer is always right'. Some booksellers are so uncouth that they end up losing half their clientele, even throwing some of them out; while others are well-disposed enough to chat to you for hours about books, local restaurants, even just to give you detailed directions. You feel that if you held them up at gunpoint and filled a heavy bag with booty, they'd open the door for you, then recommend the quickest escape route. They don't necessarily want anything out of you;

they just have time on their hands, and believe that bookselling is fundamentally a social occupation. Mr Gruff, on the other hand, has heart problems; indeed it is rumoured that his doctor judged him a unique case, and to guarantee stimulation inserted not the usual pacemaker, but a cash register instead. He only has time for people who wave notes about, especially the red kind, and often not a *lot* of time for them. The time it takes, that is, to persuade them to buy something... and then it's sod off and don't come back.

The art of persuasion: there are all sorts of tricks in the trade.

'Hello. I need a present for my sister. She loves eighteenth-century poetry. Something in a binding perhaps?'

'How much would you like to spend, madam?'

'Oh... £50.'

'OK... Let's see now.' (A little rub of the hands.) 'I have this pleasing little edition of Goldsmith's poems for £35.'

'Oh that's lovely.'

'Of course, it is a little scuffed on the spine here.'

'How honest of you. I hadn't noticed.'

'Perhaps you might prefer this Thomas Gray. Standard Eton vellum. £50.'

'This one's in excellent shape.'

'As always. But it is relatively common. I mean, you may find she already has it.'

'You are being helpful.'

'Not at all.' (Truer words were never spoken.) 'On the other hand, you might like to consider this *Rape of the Lock*.'

'*Very bijou*. And such a fine grain. How much is this one?'

'The price? Ah! how forgetful of me. It's... let me see... £75.'

'Oh dear. That's rather more than ... But it is very special.'

'And it is your sister.'

'You're right. I'll have it. Please wrap it up for me.'

There is no name for this, but you might call it 'working up the scale'. There's also the opposite trick, however: working down.

'How much is that *Arabia Deserta* in the window?'
'I'm not sure. I think it's £150.'
'Hum. That may be stretching it a bit.'
'Let me just check.' (Climbs into the window, blows the dust off it, pulls it from the shelf.) 'Sorry, I was wrong, it's only £120.'

He knows damn well it is, but he's had it too long, it's a little over-priced, in fact if this chap doesn't buy it he'll reduce it still further. Now £120 still hurts, but if your victim has already contemplated £30 more, it hurts considerably less. The customer's still unsure, but definitely wavering, so it's essential to do the following:

'£120. That's certainly more reasonable. Let me think about it.'
'Perhaps you would like to see it? Editions vary considerably. This one's very nice inside.'
'Well...'
'You're under no obligation to buy it.' (Bringing it out of the window, holding it tantalisingly in mid-air.)
'Why not? I'll have a better idea anyway.'

It is not that the customer is made to feel guilty for wasting the bookseller's time; believe me, that thought wouldn't enter most people's heads at all. No, it's touching the book with his fingers, inhaling the musty smell of old paper; the more of a collector the person is, the more he is helplessly smitten. Even if he is massively in debt, and his children are being thrown out into the street, have him cradle that book and the chances are you've got him. And booksellers, too, have very little conscience. So long as the book is sold, those starving kids can take care of themselves!

Another persuasive ploy is to move books around. There is a certain brand of ceaselessly wavering customer (let's call him the old colonel) who will come in week after week and have his eye on a particular book, and yet can't make up his mind to buy it. He circles about, apparently at his ease, but he is surreptitiously checking the fourth book along, seventh shelf down, fifth column from the left: *Strategic Positioning*. Yes! Still there. And the longer it is there, the more complacent he becomes, the longer he procrastinates. If it's been there six months, it'll be there forever (in the same way that, as far as he is concerned, the war isn't really over). Until one day he comes in, does his feeble browser impersonation, sidles secretly up to his favourite slot, fourth book along, seventh shelf down and... it's not there! Some fifth-columnist, probably a Kraut or a sneaky little Nip, has invaded his territory, got there before him. He is fuming, incredulous. With far more authority than one would have previously thought possible, he marches up to the counter, left right left right, and barks out with bullet-like precision:

'Where on earth is that book?'
'And which one was that, sir?'
'Over there. Aren't I making myself clear? Seventh shelf down. Fifth column from the left.' (Of course: what other book is there in the world?)
'Oh that one.' (He knows perfectly well; he's been watching the old colonel's manoeuvres for weeks now.) 'It's been moved.'
'Moved?' (Such a concept is clearly repugnant to him, as bad as a soldier going absent without leave.)
'Yes, sir, it's in the window. Would you like to see it?'
So it hasn't been sold. What a relief! Doesn't this mean he can waver once again? No, the insecurity is too much

for him. Bad enough that the book is not where he thought it was, now it's doing sentry-duty, it could be picked off by some sniper.

'In the window be damned. Give it to me.'

'Would sir like to buy it?' (Or, because he won the war single-handed, does he expect me to make a gift of it?)

'Yes yes, I'll buy it. Is that plain enough English? Give me that book!'

And the bookseller obeys: after all, he doesn't want to have to clean out the latrines.

Even when one doesn't have a particular person in mind, moving books around can be surprisingly effective—in moderation. You see, there is a certain bookshop in the heart of London which, every three months, takes upon its shoulders the mammoth task of reciprocating its entire stock with a sister bookshop in the West of England. (I ought to stress that these shops are not especially small.) The place closes for about a week. A lorry arrives on a Monday morning, several exhausted members of staff go backwards and forwards, transferring hundreds of little square-shaped boxes from the shop to the interior of the lorry, after which it drives off. The next day it returns, and several exhausted members of staff go backwards and forwards, transferring hundreds of little square-shaped boxes from the interior of the lorry to the shop. It's a bit like watching a film in reverse. How long all this takes I don't know; I can't bear to watch them. They then spend the next few days emptying hundreds of little square-shaped boxes and transferring their contents onto the shelves. At last, on the Friday afternoon, there is a grand re-opening, usually attended by a whole array of dealers (and a few regular customers) who zip around the narrow corridors in a frenzy and find...

Very little.

The process itself is barbaric enough, but when all they have done in the end is exchange one less than glamorous collection of books for another, we have strayed into truly surreal territory. I don't doubt that they make some money on that first day, but surely not enough (a) to justify being closed for a week, and (b) to compensate for an immediately depressed stock. Within literally an hour, the establishment has been stripped of all its best books by this shoal of piranha dealers, and is once more looking ragged, depleted, bare. Up to 50 per cent of what remains are duff ex-library books. And yet the place survives. I can be as contemptuous as I like (I'm not the only one, believe me), but it does. Perhaps because it is so well placed; perhaps because the general public will buy anything, providing it's cheap enough.

Other shops have their own peculiarities: the pricing of books, for instance. First of all, the question of *where* one finds the price. This is not always on the first blank page; sometimes there's no price at all (which always makes me uneasy—is he making it up as he goes along?), and just occasionally it is lurking on the last page (but how stupid of me, and how justly indignant you are, Mr Proprietor, when you show me where it is). Far worse is the price itself. I'm not referring now to inflated so much as *bizarre* figures. I used to think £23 or £26 was strange; but with experience behind me I'm positively blasé about it, I might even flirt with £29. But £61.40... what in the name of heaven can make a bookseller suppose this is a viable possibility? I mean, is he saying the book is worth more than £60, it's better than that, not quite £65, mind, that would be pushing it, nor bang in the middle either, no, £62.50 would not be right for this particular book, this is a slippery, elusive sort of book, it deserves a discriminating price, £61.40, has to be. Doubtless it is yet another example of endearing eccentricity (this would be the kinder view).

Another notorious bookseller used to price everything in twelves—£96, £72, etc.—and if the book didn't sell (for one thing, it usually started out at twelve times too much), he would drop the price by degrees. A book might be £144 one week (truly gross), £132 the next, and so on down in stages of twelve, giving a new meaning to the phrase 'cheaper by the dozen'. Presumably he didn't sell many books at the top price; he's not in the business any more, and small wonder. Why twelves? Nobody knows. The jury's still out on that one.

Over-pricing, however, can work: sooner or later (usually later), some mug who's always been looking for that book will walk in, and will not only pay £10 instead of £5, he'll even pay £60 (twelve times too much). The book has no intrinsic worth or merit, it is actually very common, there may even be a cheaper copy of it in the shop next door, but our friend is myopic, lazy, inexperienced—whatever the reason, he will pay well over the odds for it. This being so, why not over-price everything, just on the off chance? First of all, not everyone is a mug; for another, such cupidity may alienate regular customers. It is offensive, after all, to see mutton dressed as lamb, or to revert to our canine metaphor, mongrels passed off as pure pedigrees. If a book howls, the best way to silence it is to make it so cheap that someone just *has* to collar it and lead it away. Making money out of bad books is possible then, but should be discouraged. In fact, it might be better to break even on the odd item: deliberately under-pricing should bring people back. Or just occasionally, slip a decent book into a bargain basement: someone will dig it out, know they've got a gold nugget, and keep on coming back, thinking that further 'mistakes' are possible. If he doesn't unearth another treasure, he might even buy something at the right price, just because he feels he can now afford it, having economised the last time. Logically enough, he is hooked—both psycho- and archaeologically. Punters have their own favourite hunting-grounds, and will sometimes purchase a book from their chosen haunt which they wouldn't even consider at the same price in another.

A good book, however, one you don't see too often, should be priced solidly, that way it will linger on the shelves, be seen by a large number of customers, broadcasting the fact that interesting things turn up here, considerable care goes into the choice of stock. I accept that a lot of people don't have good taste, they won't appreciate these subtleties, but I think one should cater for one's best customers, not one's worst. And if you think *that* is sanctimonious, now I'm really going to make you puke. In an age that is increasingly vulgar, commercialised, starved of culture, it is essential for the preservation of our civilised society that a few booksellers should address the needs of the discerning public, and go on selling quality books at realistic prices.

Did you fill the bucket? Good.

It could have been worse, you know: I might have started 'forging in the smithy of my soul the uncreated conscience of my race'. Now that would have been really pretentious, meriting a whole new bucket in itself. That smithy gets about though, doesn't it, in modern literature? Not just Joyce, but Hopkins visited Felix Randal at the 'random grim forge', and as for Yeats, he had a riot with a whole bevy of smithies in *Byzantium*, real characters by the sound of it. But I digress. I'm doing it deliberately, in case you were worried—a book like this is supposed to have digressions. I mean, if it was just an irrelevance, pure and simple, don't you think the publisher would have cut it out? I don't know, time was when a writer could digress to his heart's content, page after page, and his readers would have just lapped it up. But in this age of soundbites, of short attention spans, I suppose ... well ... now what was I going to say?

6

20-Odd Ways/20 Odd Ways ... to Annoy a Bookseller

It is a sad fact that while the majority of people behave reasonably well in bookshops—to the extent at least that one doesn't notice their behaviour—a sizeable minority do not. What is it about bookshops that brings out the worst in certain people? I am perfectly aware, of course, that customers would argue from the opposite point of view: what is it about selling books that makes the staff so unutterably rude? (Indeed I gave several examples of this in the previous chapter.) You must understand, however, that I've now reverted to the other side of the counter, and this will not be about people gawping at me (how could I possibly fathom their horror?), but about me gawping at them. In other words, you must forgive my ruthless subjectivity.

A bookseller is not just a public servant, he is also a person, prey to the problems and anxieties we all have, even liable at times to be tetchy and grumpy for no very good reason, and he is rendered considerably more so by some of his more difficult customers. Now the latter are individuals as well, and doubtless they, too, have rows with their partners, close encounters with neighbours, bouts of insomnia due to some wailing infant (or is it the cat stuck in the airing cupboard?), in short, all the baggage of ordinary life, and I'm sure that their bad behaviour in public can be traced to the private sphere. A woman, for instance, who is neglected by her erring husband (or indeed, conversely, one who has been spoiled rotten all her life), may well expect, when she goes out shopping, to get VIP treatment. And who's to say she's wrong? For if we turn the argument on its head for a moment, and say that a bookseller is not just a person, he is also a public servant, then he is supposed to make an effort to satisfy a customer. Absolutely. But sometimes nothing will, and it doesn't mean that madam has to convey this expectation with every look, tone and gesture of contempt. After all, you might ask your cleaning lady to do certain jobs for you, but it is not strictly necessary to trample her underfoot while doing so (for one thing she won't be around, now will she, to clean the gunge off your shoe?).

There are many other factors in bad behaviour. The frustration of not getting what you want, even if it is over a relatively minor item (often standing in for a more emotional lacuna), may be vented out on the bookseller, the herald of bad news, what with his terminal shake of the head. The perception that the man at the desk is essentially passive, is just earning his living by sitting there doing nothing, or worse, actually reading a book (shame on him, and in a bookshop too!), makes you want to spoil his pleasure, galvanise him into action. The embarrassment: there are those amongst us (and here I must ask you to suspend your disbelief) who feel uncomfortable in second-hand bookshops.

These are very sad people. They have been sent on behalf of a relative or a friend to look for something, they don't want to do it, but if they themselves ever wish to curry favour from this said friend or relative, occasionally they will make even this supreme sacrifice. It's true of the rich too, who may find the necessity of going anywhere that isn't new and swish, that isn't all high gloss and gleaming chrome, in search of an out-of-print book, extremely distasteful. And in the same category I would place those who've never read a page in their lives till now, but who suddenly require a book of self-help, a car manual perhaps, or something to improve their public speaking. They need it. After a faltering entrance, a profound look of disorientation normally associated with arrival in some foreign land, and a somewhat lobotomised stare, they ask you for the required item with a flat, expressionless delivery.

I'm quite aware that I'm being a snob myself, an intellectual snob, but I do try not to show it. And, just to put the record straight, you will find that self-same look of fear, loathing and chronic insecurity on the face of Yours Truly whenever he ventures into a (for him) correspondingly unfamiliar environment. I refer in my own case to that nerve-jangling phenomenon, the hardware shop. I am so unspeakably out of my depth in this jungle that I too, in common with these bibliophobes, carry a white piece of paper like a flag of surrender, scrawled over with very detailed instructions as to what I'm looking for. I too enter hesitantly, walk tentatively up to the counter, hold forth my protective shield, and read off, with an appalling lack of conviction, my need for a '60-watt bulb, Osram, clear and not pearl' (yes, even such an everyday item as that). I too, if this request is insufficient, and provokes a further question ('Is that bayonet or screw-top, sir?'), look at the man with horror, wriggle with discomfort, then possibly get a little stroppy just because my extraordinary ignorance has been exposed for all to see.

Well, a bibliophobe, on asking for a copy of *How to Win Friends and Influence People* by Dale Carnegie, will look dumbfounded if you then ask him if he wants a hardback or a paperback. Now most people would know the difference between the two, but then most would know the difference between a bayonet and a screw-top light bulb, and indeed I do now, I'm never likely to forget it. You see, I'm not most people, and I dare say our friendless, uninfluential bloke isn't either, in fact, it may even be true to say that most of us are not most people... er, sort of. If my deduction is correct, that the majority of us are one-offs, then this is a source of endless fascination, or, on the down side, boundless irritation—it depends who we're dealing with at the time. We should be more tolerant, remember our own shortcomings or inanities, but the fact is that sometimes we don't, it's unflattering for us to do so.

So if you really want to know how to get on a bookseller's nerves, how to make that ninth vodka from the previous evening really bite, here is a compilation of some of those questions, habits or uncivilised actions that are likely to elicit a negative response. It may start with a barely audible snarl or grinding of teeth, develop into a feral kind of yowling reminiscent of Bruce Lee, and if you're lucky enough to hit the jackpot, culminate in previously unsuspected levels of hostility, such as forcible removal, and (in the rarest cases) actual defenestration.

How do I hate thee? Let me count the ways.

- Walk up to the counter, lean right over it and breathe your essence of garlic, gum disease and rotten drains directly into my face as you make your request... then proceed to get offended should I recoil with instinctive disgust and answer you with the same tode of voice I would use if I had a cold.

- Walk *around* the counter, assume the sideways-on position of a garotter (very disconcerting, this), lean over and whisper your furtive request (often of a pornographic nature) into my ear... then proceed to get offended should I answer you still facing front, refusing to contort my neck and thus engage in unlooked-for intimacy.

- Come in out of the pouring rain and, while browsing, drip your umbrella all over the books, or, should you lack such an implement, as you are about to go out, stop right on the threshold and block the entire entrance, impeding the traffic of both incoming and outgoing customers.

- Ask for information, and when you receive a detailed, helpful reply, prove that you haven't listened to a word:

    'You don't do new books? Can you recommend a store that does?'
    'Certainly, madam. Try Blackwell's. Straight up on this side. After the lights. Three minutes.'
    'So where's Foyle's?'

- Ask for something that doesn't exist.

'Hello. I'm looking for a bookshop called Amazon.'
'It's not a bookshop.'
'Office then—they do book searches—how do I get there?'
'But that's just it. You can't... get there.'
'Is it that far?'
'[sighing] It's on the internet.'
'Interstate?'
'In-for-mation High-way.'
'Right. And how many blocks...?'
'[exasperated] Don't tell me you've never heard of cyber-space.'
'[defensively] Of course I have.'
'[wiping his brow] Thank God!'
[Pause.]
'Well... aren't you going to tell me?'
'Tell you what?'
'Where *is* Cyber Place?'

- Come in, stop dead, look around you and inquire: 'Is this a library?'

- Be one of those people who never buy anything, a professional browser, opening every book on every shelf, glancing at it for a second, then replacing it, in the wrong position of course, scrambling up the alphabetical order; or perhaps you like to lay the paperbacks flat, horizontal, on top of neat long vertical rows (am I right? thought so), you create havoc wherever you go, and when confronted with what you are doing you're so blithely unaware, you're a natural, one might say.

- Come in, stop dead, look around you and inquire: 'How much are the books? Are they all the same price?'

- Be one of those people who never pay promptly (or even at all), who put things aside in one bookshop after another, who've never got any money on them, you're always going to be paid next week, or you've got to check if you have this book already, or you're going to the theatre so you can't possibly take it with you, but you'll be back, oh yes, you'll be back, you're like a dog, you leave a trace of you wherever you go, only you mark your territory with a book instead, yes, you're a breed in your own right, a *non*-retriever.

- If you're not sure you want a book, you might find a cheaper copy elsewhere, why not hide it behind a row of books or even put it in the wrong section, so that no one can possibly buy it in your absence, and it'll be waiting for you when you return for it, or even if you don't, in which case it might be waiting there forever.

- Come in, you students of literature and philosophy, and dazzle us with your mispronunciations, corrupt our sensitive ears with Goat's *Electoral Infinity*, or Guide's *Fawkes Moneyers*, or indeed anything by Rim-board or Floor-bert; oh and let us not forget our good old friend Des Cartes (first syllable as in Essex bloke, second and third rhyming with 'parties'), a real corker this one, guaranteed to give old Rennie indigestion, he'd turn in his grave, invent a new philosophic maxim for all students to learn: 'I stink, therefore I am.'

- On the subject of which, go downstairs, why don't you, find the most obscure corner, and when you think no one is looking, listening, or, more correctly, sniffing about, let off a titanic fart; you may even prefer an audience, go on, inflict your noxious gases on some unsuspecting browser, better, defecate (as happened once) in the middle of the floor, so you didn't like our bookshop, is that what you're trying to say, I suppose a letter of complaint would be too roundabout, you go more for the direct approach.

- Swill that beer, munch those crisps, loll your lascivious tongue round that ice-cream, smoke a particularly acrid cigar, come in, why don't you, bring all your friends, have a party, it's show time.

- Stick a bolt through your eyebrow, a safety pin through your lip, or even (by all means) have your ankles or knuckles tattooed, but don't expect me to regard you as a human being (or regard you at all, if it comes to that), disabled people I have no problem with, but people who disable themselves ... Now earrings I can understand, they're traditional, even Shakespeare had one, but when the bard wrote of

> '... the blazon of sweet beauty's best,
> of hand, of foot, of lip, of eye, of brow'

I doubt very much if it was you he was 'prefiguring'.

- First of all, stroll in with a personal stereo blaring out some mind-numbing babble, that's already enough, but then, if you really want to score, proceed to make your book request with the 'music' still on, so that—this may come as a big surprise to you—when the polite, friendly bookseller answers your question, you can't actually hear what he says.

- Carry a rubber with you, and if you don't like the price of a book, rub it out, bring it to the counter, ask how much the book is, but don't be put out if the assistant is onto you, he remembers pricing that very book an hour ago, and now he's determined you shan't have it, he wants £20 for it instead of £10, let alone £5, as you were hoping.

- When I arrive at the shop five minutes early, and go in to prepare everything, be lurking outside ready and waiting, why not tap on the window with a coin to get my attention, wave at me, look at your watch repeatedly, and when your second hand reaches the twelve and it's ten o'clock precisely, rattle the shutter, stamp up and down, shout out that I'm running late, what a performance, all you lack is a referee's whistle, and why stop at that, go on, get a warrant for my arrest, why don't you?

- Dither about at closing time, hum and ha over three lousy paperbacks, ignore several polite requests to make your final purchases, then, when you finally come to pay, ask if you can write a cheque for under £5, fill it in with paralysing slowness, hand it over, fiddle in all your pockets for your guarantee card, slap your forehead, oh dear, you left it at home. It doesn't matter, sir, now surely there can't be anything else, good, yes, you're about to turn but... no, wait, what were you thinking of, you must just have an itemised receipt, listing titles, authors, dates of publication (for the accountant, don't you know). As a final reward for bending over backwards to accommodate you, assure me how much you like this bookshop, and how—oh no—you'll be coming back regularly in future, now you're working round here you can just nip in before the end, you do hope you haven't kept me. But my dear sir from what, from the rare showing of a forgotten masterpiece perhaps, or the conviviality of a dinner party with friends, what life could I possibly have outside here, good night, no, thank *you*, sir.

* * * * *

I would now like to offer some friendly advice to various nationalities. Apologies in advance to any who might find the following remarks offensive, or, God forbid, even racist, in their tendency towards caricature.

To the French
Now I know we massacre your language whenever we're on French soil, but please, when you come over here, '*il faut cultiver votre accent*', just try a little harder to master those hard Anglo-Saxon sounds, put a damper on those long vowels of yours, all that oo-ing and aa-ing, for in these post-Inspector

Clouseau times you're at a disadvantage, you can't be taken seriously, it sounds more as if you're doing a pastiche of Peter Sellers than vice versa: 'Do you nurr if you evv anysing by Shosairre?' (Chaucer, we say, let me break it down for you: Ch-or-sir, OK sir, or rather, mon-sewer, you see, it does offend, doesn't it?).

To the Australians
Hello, how am I, well I'm doing fine since you ask, in fact I'm all for being friendly, it promotes fellow feeling and so on, but really, considering we've only just met, I find it a little strange that you should know me quite so well. As for your having no worries, I'm very pleased for you, but you mustn't assume everyone else is like you, some of us do have a few things on our minds, and I don't mean *Baywatch*, so if you'll just excuse me...

To the Japanese
Now you *do* seem a bit uptight, and please remember, you can bow and grunt as much as you like, but actually what I need to know is precisely what it is you want, try and speak more fluently, these staccato noises are very difficult for a chap like me to interpret, what was that, *Blue Flock*, I'm afraid I've never heard of it, and the author, 'Tia Seriot', no, I don't know her either, sorry, she's a melican you say, what's that, oh... *Eliot*, right, and that must be *Prufrock*, yes, yes, I quite understand.

To the English
Now you're awfully polite I know, indeed you're awfully awfully, but manners aren't everything, all this prim and proper restraint, there's also such a thing as saying what you think, though whatever you do don't mix the two together—fuck you, my good man! And another thing, it's not good to be so insular, to be forever pruning the privet, don't shut your eyes and think of England, there's a whole world out there, explore other countries, but remember (because your ancestors apparently forgot this), to explore does not mean to govern, oh you will

always be imperious, I quite understand, but don't be so goddam imper*ial*.

* * * * *

Now you would be very naïve if you thought the above were the *only* procedures for annoying a bookseller. Customers move in mysterious ways, and if I listed them all, this book would be twice its length. Before you cry out 'List away, we want our money's worth', let me add that I don't wish to be termed misanthropic and use this space as a mere customer-bashing exercise (not much!). But I would like to conclude this personal self-indulgence by devoting special attention to an entirely new area.

There are people, you see, who walk into bookshops not only with no intention of buying anything, but who don't even have books on their mind. Who are these alien creatures? Well, I wasn't going to say anything, but since you keep prompting me, there are those amongst us who use such places as a backdrop for personal relationships. Are you getting warmer, or do I have to spell it out? I have been down into the basement and caught people kissing, canoodling, and on one occasion, all but humping. Worse than this, I once came across a tearful girl wandering the various rooms of the shop in a total daze, and, on questioning this unfortunate creature, discovered that she had just that minute been dumped (which comes naturally after 'humped'). I almost shared her horror: dumped—in a *bookshop*—what will the world come to next? Now in a department store, maybe, in a shopping mall, definitely (these Kafka-esque confines practically demand the dumping of a girlfriend), but as for a bookshop, that's just getting plain nasty. I'm sure in her innocence she just came in to browse, perhaps to buy something, she got her head stuck in a book (this in itself can be painful), and then... she looks about, lover boy's skedaddled, and she's gone off the whole idea.

Do you know that poor forsaken girl might not read another book for a month, for a lifetime, she might permanently associate reading with being off-guard, with the possibility of desertion? Don't you just hate men? I do. How do you women put up with them? All right, us? I'm sure I wouldn't, I'm sure that if I were a woman I'd be a lesbian, now I know all men say that, you think they're trying to be funny, but it's interesting, I don't think I've heard a woman say the equivalent, and the reason for this is surely that most men turn women right *off*. (That was another digression, by the way.)

But for my money there's something worse than either making love in a bookshop, or dumping someone—after all, in the latter case, at least Humpty-Dumpty's brought his partner into the vicinity of books, and there's a chance that before she discovers her solitary state she may have already bought one. Moreover if she's bought mine it might console her to know she's not the first person to be dumped in a bookshop; who knows but she might even have been reading this passage at the moment of enlightenment. How therapeutic! No, for me, the most blasphemous thing a man can do is the reverse: to try and pick someone *up* in a bookshop. For there are those who can't think of such places without imagining the studious, bespectacled women who inhabit them. Proper respect—let alone reverential silence—are abandoned, they use these hallowed grounds for baser hormonal purposes, and worst of all, in making their puffed-up, tail-sweeping, pigeon-like advances, they distract the intelligent female (possessing a brain instead of a penis) from her rapturous browsing. Now I don't know if these calculating Lotharios are regular abusers, mere opportunists, or, it may be, lonely globe-trotting students in desperate search for human contact; but here's one such a melican chancer who's not going to get away with it.

[This pigeon is eighteen, in a T-shirt and jeans, with pin-up good looks: wholesome teeth, arrogant jaw, quasi-soulful blue eyes. In other words a WASP, and a bothersome one at that. The girl is English, a year younger, attractive but broodingly earnest, not yet out of her shell.]

PIGEON: [angling for an opening] Excuse me, is that *Moby Dick* you're looking at?
GIRL: [looking up] Why yes, yes it is.
PIGEON: Do you know what? That's my favourite book. [Quoting over-emphatically] 'Call me Ishmael'.
GIRL: Really? Call me female, but it looks a little heavy-going to me.
PIGEON: [forgetting himself momentarily] Excuse me! I mean... right, it takes some getting used to, I guess. [Trying a new line.] What do you like reading then?
GIRL: Oh I don't know. The English classics, I suppose. Jane Austen. I like characters I can empathise with. Like Elizabeth Bennet in *Pride and Prejudice*. She's really spunky.
PIGEON: Yeah. I know what you mean.
GIRL: Have you read that then?
PIGEON: [a little lost] Well... no, not exactly. But I've always meant to. [Trying to recover ground.] It's right at the top of my list.
GIRL: [suspicious] Hmm. There's a copy here actually. [Picking it off the shelf.] There you are. Have a look. See what you think.
PIGEON: Oh I will. Gee thanks. [Flicking through it idly, with obvious reluctance.] It looks really... cool.
GIRL: [assessing this very literally] 'Cool', yes, I suppose you could say that. Poised. Well-observed. Always good-humoured.
PIGEON: [getting personal again] I can tell you've read a lot.
GIRL: Oh no. I don't think so. I enjoy reading though.
PIGEON: You're very self-effacing. I bet you've read *everything*.
GIRL: [laughing] If only. Or... no, that would be awful, then what would I do?
PIGEON: [a little puzzled] Awful? Do? I mean... yes. After all, what else is there? [Gathering inspiration.] You know, most people in the US, they've never

	even been in a bookshop! They're too busy making money, and when they're not doing that they're keeping fit, they've just got no time for culture.
GIRL:	It's sad. And to me that's exactly what reading's for. [Beginning to respond: a danger signal.] I don't just mean an escape... it's a way of slowing down, allowing the mind time to... think, to absorb something. Oh, I'm not putting it very well.
PIGEON:	[replacing the Austen surreptitiously] I disagree.
GIRL:	Maybe that's why I read—so I will be more articulate.
PIGEON:	[a gift] But you are already. In fact, you strike me as being very... sure of yourself. [Bollocks!]
GIRL:	[slightly flattered] Do I?
PIGEON:	Yeah, as if... nothing would really get to you.
GIRL:	[laughing] Oh I don't think I'm like that at all. [Pause.] What makes you say that? [Unfortunately she's young, she really does want to know.]
PIGEON:	Well... what you said just now... about being spunky... [can't you see he's missed the point?]
GIRL:	Oh, I'd like to be Elizabeth Bennet; but as for me—
PIGEON:	And your hands. [Oh my God!]
GIRL:	[such a quick gear-change she's almost left behind] My hands?
PIGEON:	'Nothing, not even the rain, has such small hands'.
GIRL:	I'm sorry?
PIGEON:	I said—
GIRL:	But that's weird. Surely you didn't make that up?
PIGEON:	[hesitating—can he get away with it?] Actually... yes.
GIRL:	What does it mean?
PIGEON:	[flummoxed] Mean? I don't know, it just came out.

GIRL: But that's remarkable. It's... poetry.
[Enter Bookseller, me in fact.]
O.J.M.: [interrupting] It certainly is. It's e.e. cummings. From *Somewhere I Have Never Travelled*... One of his love poems.
PIGEON: [resentful, naturally] Don't be absurd.
GIRL: But are you sure?
O.J.M.: Absolutely. We may even have a copy.
PIGEON: Who the hell are you anyway?
O.J.M.: Me? I only work here.
GIRL: [pointing at Pigeon] But he was trying to pass it off—
O.J.M.: Tell me about it. He probably picked the habit up from that character in *Scoop*.
GIRL: Oh. Do you like Evelyn Waugh? [She really is keen.]
PIGEON: It was *The Loved One*. You think you're so damn clever, don't you? And now you're moving in on my terrain.
GIRL: [bridling] Excuse me, but I'm nobody's 'terrain'.
PIGEON: [ignoring her now she's a lost cause] If you're so clever, what's it mean then?
O.J.M.: Let me see now. 'Nothing, not even the rain, has such small hands'. Hum. Well, it's poetry. It doesn't mean anything.
PIGEON: See!
O.J.M.: But if I had to 'translate' it, which of course would ruin it—
PIGEON: Oh of *course*.
GIRL: Let him finish.
O.J.M.: [bowing] Thank you. I'd say it was about touch: not even the rain, which falls so gently, has the light soft touch of your delicate hands.
PIGEON: Bullshit!
GIRL: But what a lovely image.
O.J.M.: I'm afraid it's not mine.
PIGEON: [moving off, muttering to himself] Bloody booksellers. They're all the same, spoiling our fun,

	shoving their superior mugs into everything...
GIRL:	I can't thank you enough.
O.J.M.:	It's all part of the service.
PIGEON:	[going upstairs, still muttering]. And I was *that* close. Am I losing my touch? I'll have to rehearse it more with Sis.
O.J.M.:	I'm on general patrol duty, making sure books are not being stolen—
GIRL:	Or author's words.
O.J.M.:	Or women's hearts.
GIRL:	[laughing] No chance of that.
	[Pause.]
O.J.M.:	You know... when you laughed just then...
GIRL:	[curious] Yes?
O.J.M.:	I don't know. You reminded me... We haven't met before, have we?
GIRL:	I don't recall—
O.J.M.:	And yet I could have sworn... that laugh... forgive me:

'Those cherries fairly do enclose
Of orient pearl a double row;
Which when her lovely laughter shows,
They look like rosebuds fill'd with snow.'

GIRL:	[exasperated] You too? Now read my rosebuds: the answer's 'no'.

7

How to Put a Customer Down

After this barrage of ignorance and abuse it's not really surprising that booksellers should sometimes seek to exact revenge. The following is a list of put-downs in dialogue situations, some of them wholly deserved, some, I concede, just a shade gratuitous. By the way, 'C' stands for customer, and not for anything ruder (for a bookseller, the word 'customer' is in any case one of the rudest words in the language); and 'B' is self-explanatory, bearing no relation at all to questions of legitimacy.

    C: Hello. I wonder if you can help me. I need your advice. I've been into every bookshop round here, but I can't seem to find any books on my subject. Have you any idea how I might go about finding them? [Pause.] Have I come to the wrong place?

    B: And the subject is?

    C: Oh. Didn't I tell you? Here am I chattering away, and I haven't even told you. [Laughs.] Do you know why that is? I've had such a negative response, I mean every time I so much as mention the word I run up against a brick wall. I'm beginning to think there aren't any books on it.

    B: That seems unlikely.

    C: [eagerly] You think so? Am I in luck then? [B just stares at him.] I'm sorry. There I go again. [Laughs.] *Taxidermy.* Now does that help at all?

    B: Well, it's a step in the right direction.

    C: Yes?

HOW TO PUT A CUSTOMER DOWN

B: However—
C: Uh-oh.
B: Unfortunately—
C: Here it comes: you don't have any either. This is seriously pissing me off.
B: That's enough of that.
C: What do you suggest then?
B: I suggest you consult a taxidermist.
C: Meaning?
B: [leaning towards him] *Get stuffed*.

(NB The standard answer to a request for books on macramé is—surprise, surprise—'get knotted'; for mazes, 'get lost'; and, I suppose, to accommodate a figure of speech that has recently become very popular, for books on reincarnation, one might retort: 'get a life'.)

*

C: [American, of course] Do you have a rest room?
B: [hands clasped together, undertaker-style] Sir, we like to think all our rooms are restful.

*

C: I'm looking for a book: it's grey, about so high, I last saw it in Alice Springs Municipal Library in 1946... or was it 1947?...
B: I see. I know it's a bit of an oversight on our part, but we don't actually have a 'grey book' section.

*

C: Excuse me, do you work here?
B: No, I just sit at the till.
C: Oh. Who shall I ask then?
B: I was being sarcastic. Of course I work here. But let's try it the other way round, shall we? I mean, what if I were to say

HOW TO PUT A CUSTOMER DOWN

to you, 'Excuse me, are you a customer?', then your reply must inevitably be: 'No, I just ask stupid questions'.

*

C: Where do I find paperbacks?
B: In the basement.
C: How inconvenient. Can you go and check a book for me?
B: I'm afraid I'm on my own, and I can't leave the till.
C: [tutting] How do I get to the basement then?
B: We generally recommend the stairs.
C: Oh dear. My legs are bad. Is there really no alternative?
B: Well, if you stand on that floorboard there, and I press this switch here, that releases a trap-door...

*

C: Can you do a discount for bulk?
B: You're certainly large, sir, verging on obese in fact, but I don't see why I should grant you special favours...

*

C: Do you have any Bibles?
B: I'm sorry, sir, we don't deal in fiction.

*

C: Do you have *Our Mutual Friend* by Thomas Hardy?
B: I'm afraid that'll be a little difficult to find.

*

C: [overdressed, gum-chewing] Why is this book so expensive?
B: On the contrary, why are *you* so cheap?

*

HOW TO PUT A CUSTOMER DOWN

C: [after a little disagreement] Do you cultivate rudeness or is it innate?

B: Now you've got me. That's a bit of a tough one. On the one hand I do have a short temper, but I like to think I bring a touch of class to it, a level of eloquence—

C: In fact, you're so rude, I'd like to speak to the manager.

B: [gulping] What?

C: Ah! Have I struck a raw nerve? Afraid of losing your job perhaps?

B: You're making a big mistake. Remember, I only work here, and think how rude *I* am.

C: The manager. Thank you.

B: As you wish. [After a shout, Manager appears, very smartly dressed.]

C: Right. Who am I talking to?

M: Mahatma Gandhi, and who the fuck are you?

*

C: [in a strident Southern belle voice, to her husband, outside the shop]. Theeus looks like the sourd of place. Whar don't we ayask thairm earf they've got li'l ol' Madame Blavatsky? Ar thank we shured, don't you? We're here nayow, we ain't found no Madame Blavatsky anywheres ayelse, we mired as wail trar. [Coming through the door, shouting.] 'Scuse me, young maiern, we was karnd of wonderin' if y'all mired hairy such a thang as a farn edition of—

B: Madame Blavatsky?

C: [grasping her husband's hand] He's *psychic*.

*

C: Have you got any books on, like, Russian history?

B: Any particular period?

C: Oh, 1917 and stuff.

B: The Russian Revolution?

C: Like, you can read my mind?

B: OK. You might find something in this section.

HOW TO PUT A CUSTOMER DOWN

C: Cool.
[Enter Second Customer.]
C2: Excuse me, have you seen my son?
B: Is he studying Russian history and the *like*?
C2: You got it in one, pal.
B: He's in there.
C2: [spotting his son, arms akimbo] Like... where were you? Thought I'd lost you.
C: Like... me too, Dad.
C2: As if.
B: [looking at the ceiling] My God! Like son, like father.

*

C: Are you serving?
B: Madam, if you mean, am I on the staff, then the answer is yes; however, as a matter of principle, I ought to inform you, I have never *served* anyone in my life, nor do I intend to start *serving* anyone in the future. I am not your servant; in short, I do not serve. Now that we've cleared up that slight irregularity, is there any way I can be of assistance? You see, even if I do not serve, I can and will assist.

* * * * *

Now the above is a list of more or less deliberate put-downs. These tend to have four possible effects: (a) humble the customer into a state of shameful silence; (b) cause him to turn on his heel and exit pronto; (c) result in a bloody nose for Mr Smart-Arse Bookseller; or (d), and most often of all, make no impact whatsoever. All of which is par for the course. But the worst situation for a bookseller is none of these; no, this distinction must be reserved for the *unintentional* put-down. 'What is that?' I hear you gasping. Well, let me come clean. (And just to show you I'm being squeaky clean, I can tell you now that the name of the author I'm about to use is *invented*.)

HOW TO PUT A CUSTOMER DOWN

It was once my considerable misfortune to be asked for the novels of Ignatius J. Higginbottom. As far as I was aware, no one had ever asked for the novels of Ignatius J. Higginbottom before, so as you can imagine, I was surprised. Delighted. On my shelves, as it happened, I had seven titles by IJH, and I had had these for as many years.

'Yes, sir,' I said, my eyes lit up by a manic glint. 'I think I can help you.'

Trying (unsuccessfully) to keep the spring out of my step, I practically leapt over to the 'H' fiction shelf, and pulled them out. Turning away from the customer for a moment, I gave a surreptitious blow along the top edge, partly to remove the dust for his benefit, partly so that he wouldn't know how long I'd had them. I put them down on the desk; the man barely looked at them, just nodded and said he would take them all.

'But you haven't checked the prices,' I observed.

'That's OK.'

'Very good,' I said, and it was, I could barely contain my glee.

I made a mental note never to stock Higginbottom again. Seven years is a long time, and this customer, keen though he was, might never come in again, might even have completed his Higginbottom collection.

But there's something about joy that makes you talk too much.

'They're quite cheap anyway,' I went on. 'You see, there's not much call for Higginbottom yet.'

'Is that right?'

'Perhaps you might start a trend.'

He produced a tight-lipped smile.

'That'll be £35.'

'Can I use a credit card?'

'But of course.'

My tone said, yes, anything, just as long as it's real money and these books are out of my shop and out of my life. Period.

I put it through the PDQ machine. The Higginbottom collector stooped to sign it; as he seemed to take a long time, I started counting the liver spots on his bald dome of a head. One, two, three... I checked his signature against the card, and was about to hand it back to him when the name registered, I held it for a milli-second too long. Of course, you've guessed, and long before I did, that this was Ignatius J. Higginbottom Esq. in person, buying extra copies of his work for his most avid readers (i.e. himself and his friends). As he returned the card to his wallet, he gave me a level stare, knowing that I knew now, and that my previous remarks must be causing me severe indigestion. And yet he neither gloated in, nor was embarrassed by, my embarrassment.

'Thank you,' I said, as he picked up his bags. Mercifully, I didn't add anything creepy like 'I'm sure they're very good', 'I'd really like to read one of your novels', or 'Cheer up, at least you're in print'.

'Thank *you*,' he said. After all, he was pleased to find them, and if he didn't know he fell short of best sellerdom, who would?

What a nice man. I mean, would I react as equably as Higginbottom if, on entering a bookshop and asking for *Second-Hand Books: a First-Hand View*, I was presented with multiple copies at some nominal charge, and a look of intense relief on the part of the management? I hope so. Or maybe it would all be too much for me, maybe I'd start to lose control...

'Is this the one? Let me put my glasses on. [Reading the title out loud, slowly and clearly, for the benefit of all the customers.] *Second-Hand Books: a First-Hand View*, yes, that's the fella, you see, somebody recommended it to me. [To the assistant.] Have you read it? You haven't? In that case perhaps you might like to read a copy too, after all I don't need all of these, what do you say, I'll leave one for you. No no really, if what my friend tells me is true you might find it amusing. Oh all right then, look, *take* a copy, I'll pay for it, you can't say fairer than that. Now listen, you don't seem to understand, I insist that you read it, that's right, you heard me correctly, let me just sign it for you,

you see, I'm the author. Oh you guessed that already, did you, well you'll have to agree I'm in a unique position, I know the book inside out and I can recommend it wholeheartedly, and now that I've signed it it'll be more valuable. But my dear chap, it's not a question of choosing what you read, I'm choosing it for you, here, let me wrap it up for you, now if that isn't a grand gesture I'd like to know what is, I bet that doesn't happen too often, eh, a customer serving a bookseller? But what do you mean no, I'm putting myself out here, what can you possibly still have against it? Now really there's no need to be silly, call the police indeed, I'm being perfectly reasonable aren't I, surely *you're* the one, I mean, you're deliberately defying me, you might at least have pretended you were going to read it, that's what any decent person would... Look, let's be civilised about this, I am *not* causing a scene, just ask anyone here, ask... ask... oh what's the matter with you all...'

And maybe not.

To conclude on a positive note, though I came out of it badly, the Higginbottom experience was also a liberating one. By this I mean it is actually possible to *please* a bookseller: not just by spending a lot, taking your purchases away immediately, or even just accepting that he hasn't got the book you want. No, the best way to do this is to have a taste for the unfashionable, for those books that don't exactly jump off the shelf—even the poltergeists won't touch them. Spend £50 on these, and you'll be doing him a bigger favour than spending £200 on quality. Not that, after this chapter, you'd ever want to do him any kind of favour—perhaps you'll never enter another bookshop again.

8

Begging, Stealing or Borrowing

But people don't just go to bookshops to buy books (or indeed to waste their time and yours); they also come to sell (or not, as the case may be). Now the main reason for the failure to sell a book is that the commodity on offer is of no intrinsic interest. For instance, it might be useful for you to know that shops are rarely interested in the following: paperbacks underlined with marker pen; mass-produced book club editions; ex-library copies (even with the 'withdrawn' stamp); worn-out travel guides smeared with the blood of every mosquito you swatted on your last holiday; or obscure technical books: whether it be a sex manual for astronauts—limited options, of course, during weightlessness in outer space—or a companion to how to play water polo while balancing a basket of fruit on your head.

No, these and other such everyday items are not wanted, so it is no use standing there in disbelief for ten minutes insisting they must be desirable just because *you* got something out of them. Even if you think the buyer is wrong, he is the umpire, technically you are 'out', so don't linger at the crease. Booksellers get enraged when their decades of experience are initially called upon, only to be summarily swept aside by the layman when the verdict is not what he wants to hear. If, after blanket rejection, you still believe your coronation programme is as precious as an illuminated manuscript, you might as well keep it—indeed, you've got little alternative. Or, if you really think you know better, set up your own bookshop, try and sell the kind of dross that you offer, and just see how long you last in business. Of course, many do precisely this, and they find that even before the sign painter's finished glossing over 'Books of Ours', another chap's come along to whitewash the windows.

As I say, in order to sell something successfully, the vital ingredient is the book itself. But it isn't everything. There is also such a thing as presentation. Now it is true that even a flawless technique is not going to help you sell a commercial dud; no fast talking, arm-twisting, or brilliantly inventive hard luck stories are going to transform the object into something other than it is. But presentation can help in those borderline cases when the book is saleable in a modest sort of way, is in so-so condition, or is a duplicate of something the buyer already has.

What is good presentation? This is difficult to say. But I may arrive more easily at an answer (and have a good deal more fun in the process) if I first discuss *bad* presentation. There are some classic opening lines that are guaranteed to make a bookseller immediately uncomfortable; on uttering any of the following little gems, you can almost guarantee that the light will go out of his eyes, the hairs start to bristle on the back of his neck.

'I don't suppose you'll be interested...'

'I was clearing out my attic the other day, and I found this book, it looked a dead ringer for one I saw on *The Antiques Roadshow*...'

'I've got loads of books here, they're cluttering up my flat, give me a price for the lot...'

'I hear you buy books. Is that all kinds? I mean, do you buy *anything*?'

'Can I speak to the buyer please? I've got something rather special, and I don't want to waste my morning dealing with somebody inexperienced...'

It is not merely a question of what you say or how you say it (from the sepulchral tone of the first example—a man with the word 'loser' emblazoned in fiery letters on his forehead—to the overbearing toff at the other extreme); it can be even such a factor as the way you walk. Some people literally creep up to the counter, eyes half-staring at you, half-looking away, and when they reach down into their bag it's with such unbearable diffidence that the words 'sorry, not for us' are on your lips before you've so much as seen the book. (When Empson said 'learn a style from a despair', I don't think he had this in mind.) Others are too sprightly, practically dance up to you with their proffered item, and while you're inspecting it, try to soft-soap you into a good mood by asking how business is; but they soon find themselves dancing out again, keeping up the pretence even as they vacate the premises. One thinks of Monty Python's 'Always look on the bright side of life', and it is only too true that trying to sell a book can be a crucifying experience. Essentially what you are doing is asking for money—you're offering something in return, but it's still a glorified form of begging, and like that pastime, involves a huge amount of negative feedback. Even when you've got the right book at the right price, you could still be told 'I'm afraid we've got one already', or 'We've bought too much this week'.

The result: if you've spent the last hour girding up the courage to sell the book in question, you've basically got to go through it all again with someone else. Indeed, it's such a humiliating ordeal I sometimes wonder if it's worth it. Profit is a powerful motivator, but I suspect that for many people the first time they try to sell a book is often their last.

I have touched on the importance of what you say and how you move in these borderline cases, but there's still a third factor: receptacles! For it really can be off-putting to the buyer if you lift up to the counter one of those cheap, wafer-thin, faintly malodorous supermarket bags and set up an interminable rustling while you forage for the book that's inevitably got stuck at the bottom. Or, once again at the other end of the spectrum, if you slam your attaché case down, fiddle around with various combination locks, make all the requisite clicking noises that are so officiously self-important, and then remove from this portable

Fort Knox... a large ball of newspaper, proceed to unwrap this slowly, layer by layer, as if it were an Egyptian mummy, take out... a smaller piece of tissue paper, peel back several strands of Sellotape, and then present the remarkably patient bookseller—though his fingers may be observed drumming on the till—with... a Flemish–Hungarian dictionary!

As in so many things, simplicity is best. Don't show a lack of confidence, because then even if the book is of some value, it is quite possible that a hawkish bookseller may offer you less than he might; and if you come on too strong, antagonising the buyer from the start, he may well end up sacrificing potential profit to a greater desire to give you nothing at all. The best way to offer a book, then, is to be straightforward and direct, to regard it as a business transaction, and await a verdict patiently, unembarrassed, without pacing up and down like a father-to-be. It's probably best to meet the eyes of the buyer with a certain candour, show that you're alert, and not some wide-eyed, cloth-capped provincial happy to stand there gormlessly while he tightens the noose round your neck. If you know what you're talking about, make the odd observation; if you don't, keep your mouth shut, or he may call your bluff and find you out. Don't give away your ignorance; conversely, don't assume that the buyer is a fool either.

Of course, it is quite possible that the buyer is a fool or, more likely, not entirely straightforward himself. Despite the general bias of this book in favour of the trade over and against the general public, I would be the first to admit that booksellers are people too, businessmen above all, and they want the best deal they can possibly get. I would not tar them all with the same brush, but some, shall we say, are less generous than others, and a few, well, might have made excellent pawnbrokers. If they have regular suppliers, they soon get to know those who have a low opinion of themselves in general and their books in particular, or those who have a cannier estimate of their worth, and they will adjust their offer accordingly. As for the third category, the ones who push too far in the other direction, always making a fuss, and sometimes too vocally, once they're identified they're unlikely to be granted a future audience.

One general point: with experienced buyers and sellers there is often a battle for the middle ground. Power games revolve around two essential questions: the seller can ask 'How much will you give me?', and the buyer can reply 'How much do you want?' Or vice versa. This mutual reconnoitring, or just plain shilly-shallying, can go on for quite a while, until one or the other adversary surrenders in a war of mental attrition.

B: But you must know what you want.
C: I want the best price you can offer.
B: And what might that be?
C: Surely that's for you to say.
B: Well... you know, that was almost quite clever.
C: I nearly had you there, didn't I?
B: It was close, I admit.
C: But not quite close enough?
[B just smiles.]
C: Look, what would you say to £80?
B: What would you say to 60?
C: Damn!

The point being, of course, that if the seller is forced to state his price, and it happens to be a little low, or less than the buyer was prepared to spend, the latter can swoop down on him quickly and agree, or undermine the price still further. On the other hand, if the buyer is forced to offer a definite figure, the seller can find himself in the stronger position: though the amount offered is already more than he had in mind, he can pretend to be a little unhappy with it, purse his lips, and try to push it up a notch or two. Certainly on making offers to some individuals I have noticed a transitory look of shock in their eyes—now have I offered too little or too much? Subsequent remarks ('That's more or less what I expected') or sounds (a leonine purr) often clarify the situation.

Now if you are a seller and you know your books and you find the buyer really doesn't know what he's talking about, or is trying it on, evaluating what fraudulent price he can get away with, there is good reason for you to be angry. But ranting and raving against—what shall we call him?—Mr Ripoffsky is probably a mistake. For one thing, this is his establishment, it was your idea to cross his threshold, nor can you prove anything against him. The best way of handling a low offer is to chuckle quietly to yourself, shake your head, put the book away, turn promptly on your heel and go out, perhaps still quietly sniggering, and certainly ignoring any further overtures from the humiliated owner. For it is quite possible that, perceiving his bluff has been called, Ripoffsky will attempt to up the price, once, twice, to become quite importunate, in fact. Do not deal with this man, he doesn't deserve to gain from your merchandise, find a more reputable dealer.

Do I hear an ironical aside from the more cynical-minded readers at this juncture, that Ripoffsky is just a thinly disguised version of myself? No, I'm being paranoid, for how can you have known that I do indeed have some Eastern European blood? Whoops! As a matter of fact I have always been fair in my dealings with people, my nose may be long but it is not getting any longer as I write these lines (this paper smells nice), so if you ever want an honest offer for a book, please give me a call on...

[We feel it is in the interest of public health and safety that Mr Davis' number be withheld at this point. We acknowledge that this is done without the author's permission, we take full responsibility for our actions, but we don't believe he should make commercial gains out of this book.][1]

[[This is entirely consistent with their policy of paying me the smallest possible advance—talk about stingy!]][2]

So who are these sellers? People like you and me, involved in the ordinary upheavals of everyday life, whether it be moving from a house to a flat, or tidying up the affairs of a dead

---

[1] Publisher's note
[2] Author's note

relative, or, as I mentioned earlier, selling off one collection to finance another. Then there are tourists who come all the way from Australia with a book to sell (don't they have bookshops in Australia—no, perhaps not), or those who are returning there and don't want to heft anything back (even if it is essentially *light* reading); students who have finished their courses and need some cash as they go out into the real world (this being a place where books no longer have to be read); members of the book trade itself, who have perhaps acquired a few items outside their area of specialisation; book runners—

Book runners? These are rather nebulous characters who don't have a shop or stall or any kind of retail outlet, nor do they issue lists or catalogues. They have usually at some time or other worked more conventionally for another dealer, learned the trade, picked up a mine of information, and now prefer to use that knowledge in their own peculiar way. Book runners are not nine-to-five people, the daily grind of slow cumulative profit and trading with the general public (I can't understand this) are not for them. They're will-o'-the-wisps, restless, impatient, flitting from bookshop to auction house to book fair, covering an enormous amount of ground, a case of now-you-see-him-now-you-don't, or even of appearing to be in two places at the same time.

And what are they doing all the while? Basically their *modus operandi* is to be continually aware of which book is in which location, to pick up various people's requirements on the way, whether it be dealers or private punters, and to try and match the two up. The runner knows, for instance, how one shop has a customer who will pay over the odds for a Ralph Steadman collection because he's one of the subjects caricatured; another has a direct order from the sultan of some Arab state for a St John Philby travel book; while a third needs volume two of the *Dance to the Music of Time* sequence by Anthony Powell to complete the whole run—and urgently, for a rival bookseller in an identical situation may get there first. (Now if this second dealer uses the same runner, things could turn quite nasty.) If he has seen or heard of any of these books on his travels, he can then report back with a quote. For this reason runners are often able to buy things at the 'right' price (books that the trade would not normally touch) and still move them on at a tidy profit, though just as often they make money out of mistakes. Some have been known to go abroad to get the book they want (in the case of America, I suppose it's more a question of swimming); while there are tales of others buying a book in one shop, crossing the road, and then selling it to the dealer opposite, making £500 in thirty seconds.

Runners, then, are street-wise to a T, and have more eyes than Argus, but if they're spending a lot they'll need to double-check that the book is still required, so they will tend to put things aside, dash out to use their mobiles, and then return with a thumbs-up or thumbs-down. Some are simply risk-takers, and for this reason, and their lack of a regular turnover or dependable income, they can have financial problems. Runners' cheques have something in common with trampolines; booksellers will often demand payment in cash. Where they get the cash from is another matter... perhaps they go to the nearest market trader, sell the shirt off their back, clinch the deal, and then retrieve it. They're an exotic breed, one that is dying out, for we live in the age of the internet and the book fair, where everyone seems to know the latest prices, bargains are fewer and further between, and rival dealers tell each other their latest wants, thus cutting out the middleman. They're a law unto themselves, but while they break every rule, often infuriate with their comings and goings (they *cannot* keep still), they have a certain charm, style, panache. This is the more positive view. Some booksellers, it has to be said, fall foul of them, and stories of books being taken 'on approval', of debts that remain outstanding, are not uncommon in the trade, for runners can bluff their way with real conviction.

Talking of conviction, there is another kind of runner, and this is the kind who runs from the law. Something like a third of all books offered to shops on a daily basis are stolen. How does one determine this? The more experienced one is, the easier it becomes. Most booksellers know before the chap has so much as stepped through the door. For a start, thieves tend not to walk like ordinary people; there is a certain width to them—they loiter, shuffle or swagger aggressively. Their opening line is invariably in-your-face ('Yer buy books mate?'); there is a singular lack of finesse about their approach. Other give-away lines include: 'None of 'em 've ever been read', 'They're all unwanted presents' and 'I don't want much for them'. Ironically, if they asked for the right sort of money, a percentage of the actual value, one might be less suspicious; by asking so little they reveal both their ignorance and their desperation. They have an air about them, tough, confrontational, brutalised by life whether in or out of prison. They wear rough clothes reeking of roll-up cigarettes, hard floors and doss-houses. They convey life lived in the raw, on the edge, where the luxury of reading would be an irrelevance. Books are the one thing they should *not* try to sell; books and they do not belong together.

It is not that they are stupid... no? I may be condescending, a prodigious snob, but if I want to be honest I have to say these people are stupid, or a lifetime of deprivation has made them so, because so often they make no effort to convince you they're straight. If they're not rude and aggressive enough, if the books aren't absolutely pristine (with the shop's sticky label still attached to them), then there's the way they look at you—pinpoint, shining, smack-happy eyes—or avoid visual contact altogether. Perhaps it's not so much a question of being stupid; more a matter of being so unavoidably themselves. They don't know how they sound or look to me, how they exude dishonesty out of every pore, any more than I know just how effete and bourgeois I must sound to them. Doubtless they'd pronounce it 'borgias'. You see? There I go again. They might say that all I can do with my superior education is make poisonous remarks like that. Still we are what we are, and they're at a double disadvantage, because I've also got the power of refusal, and I'm not going to buy their books at any price.

But I think I was right in the first place. Is it not, after all, stupid to offer me a clutch of some twenty brand-new Penguin paperbacks (Calvino, Camus, Carter, Cary etc.), all starting with the same two letters, and so clearly the victims of a single swipe; is it not stupid to say you have a book for sale, and on being asked what it is, look puzzled, take it out, and read off the title with halting illiteracy; is it not astonishingly stupid to nick a book from *my* shop, try all the other dealers in the vicinity, fail to sell it, and then come and offer it back to me as a last resort? Either they're so full of junk they've forgotten where they got it in the first place, or, who knows, it might be they make up in sheer nerve what they lack in brain.

Some thieves are actually so inept, I end up feeling sorry for them. I have caught more than one drunk standing right in front of me, attempting to manoeuvre an unwieldy book beneath his balloon-like shirt with startling, sorry, staggering inefficiency. I have gone up to these individuals (though not too close—you can die of passive drinking) and received a look of utter disbelief. What? You saw me? No, they don't know what they're doing—*I've* got a better idea of what they're doing—and for this they must be pitied. Needless to say, some are more harmless than others, some get quite nasty when you turn them away ('D'yer think I'm a thief or something?'), and you have to be careful how you handle them. I have never actually said 'Yes, I do think so' (why volunteer to go sailing across the room?) but I'm tempted to; anything to avoid the standard prevaricating replies: 'The buyer's not in', 'We're overstocked at the moment', 'We only buy at auction' etc. etc. They usually have a bit of form, sooner or later take no for an answer and go searching for another outlet. It's no good being really rude to them (as they often are to you); next time they might come back with a friend, even a metallic one, for hold-ups are not unknown in the book trade, especially in recent years. If it's late in the day, and there's only one person manning the till, bookshops can look like an easy target.

Perhaps one should be grateful that these incompetent thieves are only as bad as they are; there are surely much worse. And they're not all equally stupid. Some ring first (they're harder to identify without the visual confirmation), ask if you buy books, and then bring them in later, at which point it's harder to back out of the deal ('But you said on the phone...'). Or they send in a front guy (more often a woman), someone more plausibly respectable, and you might make the mistake of buying off this person. But there's something dodgy about her anxiety to please (the chances are, a girlfriend of a criminal will have picked up some of his shiftier mannerisms by personal osmosis); and if you look carefully enough, you can see her accomplice hovering restlessly outside (he's in dire need of a fix). Thieves often work in pairs, one presumably as some sort of lookout, or to distract you while the other is backing a pantechnicon through your rear entrance. If you're not careful, your entire section of transport books might have turned into a library on wheels.[3]

But they're not all drunks and druggies and down-and-outs, not all underclass, not by a long chalk. While some books are hot (definitely stolen) and others warm (something just doesn't ring true about the provenance), others are positively cold. One has no suspicions whatever. The chap selling to you is in a pinstripe suit, the books are recent but he's doing some up-to-date research, if he's really clever he'll have thumbed them a little to make them look read, all in all he's so kosher it's not even occurred to you he could be anything else. And yet this man, too, is a thief. He might have picked up an expensive coke habit, or perhaps he's been made redundant from the City and has a massive mortgage to keep up—and if it's both of these, then he's really got nothing to snort about. Such 'respectable' cases are rarer, one can be forgiven for making a mistake, but they're more aggravating. Firstly, they remind you that no amount of experience will make you right all of the time; secondly, and more importantly, you realise how biased you are towards your own class, how you jump on the visibly downtrodden, but fail to perceive the threadbare morals lurking beneath a smartly dressed exterior.

And then you realise a third possibility: some of the people you assumed were thieves, just because they were rather rough and ready, failed to observe the proper protocol, or even said

---

[3]There are those, too, who don't merely smuggle books *out* of bookshops; they actually smuggle them in. I refer to our old friend the 'vanity' author. He can't get the proper distribution for his book, and so is forced to use his own ingenuity, sneaking copies onto the shelves when nobody's looking—not for commercial gain, but in the desperate hope that some intrepid reader will chance it. Nobody ever does.

the wrong thing in all innocence, may actually be straight. Not often: if you smell a rat, the likelihood is, it's dying in front of your eyes. But it's possible. Some people say too much, tell you they've got ID, and if you weren't suspicious before ... I mean, why be so defensive, if not because they've something on their conscience? Would it even occur to the innocent to show ID? But it could just be they've got an unfortunate face—Quasimodo out of Nixon—they've run into obstacles before, and they're trying to be co-operative. All the same, one should never buy a book one is not at least 95 per cent sure about; 100 per cent is more difficult. God knows, maybe all books are stolen, nobody's really honest out there, not even people who love books.

Sometimes they least of all. Bad enough to have a drug habit and steal books as a way of financing it (you could steal any other commodity just as well); but when bibliophiles steal, the book *is* the drug, it provides its own ecstatic hit. And like the other kind of offender, their habit doesn't get any less demanding in its urgency, if they're short of cash they must take more books, maybe their dosage even increases. This may sound absurd to some, but it isn't funny, or at least not for the booksellers who are the victims of such wholesale plunder. In fact, it's a worse scenario than the first, for there is no hope of a reprieve: the bibliophile is hardly going to OD, he can ingest vast quantities of knowledge without any damage to his health. Nor is he easy to pin down. It may even be a regular customer, someone who has bought many volumes in the past, who gets a special discount, and with whom one's on first-name terms. This man is ill; if he can't die of his particular habit, he is out of control, his sense of decency is being undermined. Fortunately he's not common, I won't say rare, though when he turns up he's invariably in a jacket (slightly frayed at the edges).

Most regular customers, however, are ordinary, honest, respectable, even if they ask for a discount and are refused, they're not going to turn round, help themselves, and walk out with backs a good deal squarer than when they came in. The offending bibliophile (like his paedo- equivalent) is just as likely to have strayed in from another area. He is not regular, not local, but a tourist perhaps, unknown territory.

BEGGING, STEALING OR BORROWING

I remember one extraordinary case. This was an American doctor who collected antiquarian books. What does he do? Firstly, he looks at the bindings by the till; secondly, he makes a tour of the whole shop, checking out all the other rooms; finally, he works his way back to his starting-point, scans the bindings again, picks out an old medical book for £150, and pays for it. While this is going on, he is chatting to us, he is informed and agreeable, not in the least bit suspicious, he even says he'll contact us with a wants list. He picks up his package and leaves.

Ten minutes after he's gone, quite casually one of us notices a book has strayed in among the bindings, not that far from the gap left by the doctor's purchase, one of the same brown colour as its neighbours, but actually a modern cloth book from a different section. At first we're merely puzzled, thinking that someone has put it back in the wrong place, not even realising the sinister implications (it must be standing in for *another* binding), and least of all connecting it with our doctor friend. Then, attempting to replace this brown cloth book where it belongs, several shelves away from the bindings, we notice there's no gap there, yet another book has been moved from still another section to fill the place of *this* one. We're getting worried; two such anomalies smack of the underhand, the premeditated; and by now we've worked out which leather binding is unaccounted for. As we transfer this second misplaced item to its natural habitat, in a different room from the bindings altogether, there we find the gap (and not, as we hope, our missing antiquarian book).

So what has he done? Somehow or other, this American doctor has so shuffled things around that nothing appears to be missing, has stolen a book from right before our eyes, for all we know while he was talking to us, even while purchasing the other. Precisely how or when he did this is difficult to gauge. Perhaps he distracted us momentarily while pointing to a book higher up, or maybe he didn't even need to do this, and it was done *after* his purchase. He'd lulled us into such a false sense of security we didn't even notice that split second's sleight-of-hand, that quicksilver reciprocation of one book from his pocket to the shelf with another from the shelf to his pocket. Or he might have done it in separate stages. Whatever the truth, he was so successful that a leather binding worth £300 had vanished into thin air, and the culprit with it. And doubtless, professional that he was, confident in his tried and trusted technique, he must have walked out at his leisure, only bolting when he had safely turned the corner.

This man was not a thief, at least in conventional terms; he genuinely wanted the book he paid for, and could presumably afford it; but he equally wanted this other more expensive book, he was even prepared to risk cutting short his illustrious career, and incurring a jail sentence to boot. (Mind you, he was so dexterous he probably would have stolen the keys and escaped!) Unlike all the thieves I've mentioned above, this man was clever, extraordinarily so. In fact, he had turned thieving into an art, one of military precision, a perfectly planned kidnapping and subsequent cover-up, aided and abetted by an elaborate camouflage operation. I suppose the medical equivalent would be to sweet-talk you into thinking nothing was wrong while simultaneously amputating your little finger. And this rare breed of larcenous bibliophile, with his educated demeanour and insidious technique, is the hardest to identify. He is capable of stealing not only the odd book when desperate, but dozens, hundreds of books from shops all over the country, and further, a record as bad as any indiscriminate burglar.

But the story doesn't end here. As I said before, this man is not simply a thief, he knows the difference between right and wrong; he can't stop himself, it is true, but he suffers for it. Why am I being so corny, so Hollywooden all of a sudden? Well, in this particular case—I doubt if it is typical—there was an unexpected epilogue.

I think it must have been some three years later that a mysterious package arrived. At first, on opening it, and perceiving an antiquarian book, I was merely puzzled. Such items don't normally turn up out of nowhere, and it had been so long since it was filched the title was almost unfamiliar. Then I remembered. There was nothing else with it, no covering letter or note of apology, just the book itself, none the worse for wear, in the state in which he had stolen it. Very clinical, you might say. Should I have been angry (at having such a humiliating memory revived) or grateful (well, it *had* come back, and if anything it was worth even more now than when it disappeared)? Whether he had extracted full bibliophilic pleasure from it and was sated enough to return it, or had made enough money now to purchase his own copy, or had had a belated change of heart, who knows? Maybe it was nothing so laudable, the police were onto him and he knew it, and he was desperately getting rid of the evidence in advance of a raid, frantically sending off packages all over the world to their rightful destinations. Or wrongful. If we assume a mass plunder, and a less than perfect memory, he might be sending *The Anatomy of Melancholy* to a humour specialist, or a history of vegetarianism to a dealer in blood sports.

Never mind the morality, we were just glad to have it back. If he'd walked in, we probably wouldn't even have prosecuted him—pinned his hands behind his back, yes, if only to avoid a repeat performance. Personally, I didn't even begrudge the high it must have given him. And that's the nice thing about books. They can be bought and sold over and over again, change hands many times, and give spiritual (as well as financial) reward to many. Even a flimsy paperback can go on a circuitous journey through a series of miscellaneous owners during its comparatively brief lifespan...

9

The Journey of the Book

My name is *Oranges Are Not the Only Fruit*, a bit of a tongue-twister I admit, so if you like you can call me 'Oranges' for short. Like all books, I have only one parent—no, that's not true, I met *Diary of a Nobody* once and it had two daddies, and then there was *An Irish RM* and that had two mummies. Well, I had a mummy too, only one, and in terms of novels at least, I was her first-born. My mother is a writer—surprise, surprise—yes, I think I can say that all my acquaintances had writers for parents. As it happens, she's a very successful one, but this has not necessarily been to my advantage. Certainly I have been sought out, but often, it seems to me, for the wrong reason. While I personally have nourished the heart and mind of at least one reader, I have also been bought and sold by many, used and finally abused, and this is why I lie here moribund, my life's print ebbing out of me.

Like all books, I never really knew my mother, though I'm told I resemble her to an extraordinary degree. My first clear memory is of springing into the world out of Pandora's box. Soon I was taken from the warehouse of this publisher and put out for adoption—i.e. inhabiting the fiction shelves of a new bookshop in London. It was a bit of a supermarket, but at least they kept it clean; besides, I had good company, we were all young, glossy-complexioned, and full of dreams. Our common aspiration, we agreed, was to stimulate the lives of humans. No one showed much interest at first, but occasionally someone would come along and ruffle my pages; I was put smartly back. I suppose many were put off by the subject-matter—I believe I am quite controversial—though this is nothing to do with me; I mean, you can't judge a book by its contents.

Sometimes it worked the other way. One or two people browsed through me with what I can only call a certain prurience—a bloke in a leather jacket with close-cropped hair, actually I'm not sure it was a bloke, and another one, definitely male, for his excitement was visible, if you know what I mean. This was not the kind of stimulation I had in mind. I don't know if you have any experience of it, but it's horrible being treated as a sex object, especially as I'm so unsexy myself. Like all my kind, I'm entirely neutral and passive, I may be called 'Oranges' but I'm not in touch with my sex-a-peel. Desire, too, is an alien concept: what use is desire to a book? A book is a world, after all, self-contained, cerebral, why should it consort with other worlds? How?

Eventually one woman lingered longer over me, handed over a couple of pounds or so (I am only a paperback), and before I knew it I was held in her tight grip on the way to my first real home. I don't wish to sound spoiled or ungrateful, but after my spacious beginnings her Brixton flat seemed a rather poky affair, not decorated to a very high standard. To be honest, she wasn't well off, and this was perhaps reflected in her sparse library. But if she was a casual reader, this woman, Cara, was serious about me, she didn't just toy with my pages, she was the first to read me from cover to cover. (Or to take my virginity, I believe you humans say.) She read me carefully too, without dog-earing the corners, which as you know can leave a permanent scar. She was in her mid-forties, gaunt, prematurely grey, with a clenched mouth, and chewed-over lips. But she had extraordinary eyes, vocal, importunate, probing in their fixity. I should know. For while humans can read me, simultaneously, I can read them.

If the truth be told (and naturally, as a book, I feel compelled to speak the truth), I think the story meant something to her personally. She had missed the boat as far as sex was concerned, she had never officially come out, she was afraid of love, or at least the kind she had to offer. Once or twice she brought friends back for a coffee, she used to sit very tensely with them, but they never stayed over; in fact, when she saw them out, I noticed, she didn't so much as peck them on the cheek. Only when they'd gone, she'd sit down and wring her hands, and start acting out the scene all over again, this time declaring herself openly. And yet, strange to say, late one night when a friend did lean over during one of those difficult silences and kiss her, once, smack on the lips, Cara's face became a conflagration, she panicked, started shouting, and threw her out.

She was so repressed that I think eventually it consumed her. I'd been with her several years when she suddenly got ill. The flat was empty for a while; then she shockingly returned, shaven-headed; thinned to a wedge, transitional; vanished. The flat was empty even longer. Dust settled on me like ashes. Weeks unhappened before someone else came to clear away her personal effects.

Hers was a sad sort of unresolved existence, but I take comfort from the fact that she prized me above all else. How do I know this? Well, she took me once to a new bookshop where my mother was signing her latest effort, and asked if she wouldn't mind signing me instead. Mummy willingly complied. That was the only contact I ever had with her—weird to feel her caressing me with her pen—no, I can't say we were really bonded. I was then taken home again, and treasured even more as a result.

Yes, she read very little: when her sister came to sort out her library, there were only forty-odd paperback novels and a meagre array of reference books. What followed was very degrading. I was tossed any old how into a PVC bag with all the others, taken by car to the nearest charity shop, and dumped there. A singularly dim-witted man at the counter plodded through us one by one, gave a brief glance at the price on my back, and then scribbled in a modest '50p' inside my front cover. I must say I felt humiliated: even paperbacks have feelings. This was a dingy establishment that smelled insidiously of puke and unwashed clothes, and was frequented by an altogether poorer class of person. My life, I felt, was on a downward spiral; how I longed to be rescued.

I didn't have long to wait. A dark-skinned man in a head-wrap came in, scanned the shelves, took hold of me, looked at my price, and bought me. He dropped me into a carrier bag; but far from finding myself alone with only plastic for company, I was surprised to land on others of my kind from a previous catch, smarting under the thud of my arrival. Then we were all taken for a long walk during which further charity shops were visited and yet more orphaned paperbacks were bundled in on top of me. When at last he had finished his trawl, we got a bus back to his flat in a curious hinterland called Nine Elms, where I was greeted by an unfamiliar smell—curry. Now while I find no smell at all appetising, at least this was better than puke.

My new owner, who was called Mr Singh, was very different from my previous one; where she had been solitary, he was gregarious, indeed he often entertained other men in head-wraps. From what I gathered, these were called turbans, and all the men who wore them Mr Singh, which I found rather puzzling—I mean, aren't names supposed to identify you? Not many books, after all, are called *Oranges Are Not the Only Fruit* or even 'Oranges' for that matter. They came from India—well, all I can say is, directory enquiries must be chaos there. Name please?—Mr Singh—initial?—T—there are 32,000 listed, sir, are you really looking for T. Singh, just plain T. Singh, or are you... just plain teasing? (Oh dear. It fell rather flat, didn't it? My friends always said I had a lousy sense of humour.)

The first Mr Singh did various odd jobs, and supplemented his low income by dealing in paperbacks as a sideline. He had picked up what little he knew from a friend who used to run a junk shop in Vauxhall. In fact, I had only been at his place for a week when this friend (a Mr Banerjee, I was relieved to hear) came round and glanced through his latest haul, offering 80p a book. Mr Singh, it seems, worked on a very small mark-up. If what he paid for me was typical, then he made about 30p each—he would need to buy a hundred just to make £30. Such dedication: that one circuit, the day he bought me, had taken hours. Well, small pleasures as they say, and apart from the exercise I think he enjoyed the hunt.

Mr Banerjee didn't waste any time: he drove straight to the nearest second-hand bookshop, parked his car outside, and unloaded. A man at the desk went through us all systematically, and paid him an average of one pound each. Mr Banerjee's mark-up was even less then, only his part in all this was easier, he didn't do any of the leg-work. Knowledge must be a very pleasant thing; it saves you aching limbs. Not that I would know anything about that of course, I who am always carried wherever I go. Now why Mr Singh didn't take us straight to the bookshop himself is anyone's guess. Being a modest, unassuming man, maybe he didn't have the confidence to deal with what he might have called the big time—he needed a middle man. And the middle man didn't have the patience to run a shop any more, where he might make a better profit in the long run, but preferred to make money quickly up front.

Now you would think, wouldn't you, that after this trade-off, having arrived in a second-hand bookshop, I am bound to end up in another reader's home. You see, I've only been read the once, and every book wants to be appreciated. Like the man in the charity shop, like Mr Singh and Mr Banerjee, the buyer in this place gives me a cursory glance (he has scores of us to price), and scribbles '£3' in his own hand, something like half the price I would now be in a new bookshop. Despite having been passed around like an African slave, I'm in reasonable condition. He places me alphabetically under W (it seems I'm not allowed my *own* identity), in company with books like me who have seen a bit of the world, have been soiled or roughed up, a less reputable class than the new ones with whom I shared my infant experiences.

As the customers scan the shelves, I scan them. Who will be my next owner? Who would I prefer? Not this gentleman, I hope—he's so dour and pale and unhealthy—no, a shake of the head and he puts me back. He asks the owner where the cookery books are—so that's what he took me for. Damn fruitarians! Next a girl picks me up, she looks like the penniless student type, which makes me visualise further domestic squalor. She hums and has, perhaps she's weighing up whether I'm cost-effective: she might almost prefer to buy a pristine copy at full price for keeps (when she's better off), and meanwhile buy the scruffiest, cheapest possible copy to read. Yes, yes, I'm willing her as she puts me back. Then an older woman looks at me, with a certain disapproval I might add, but also a touch of curiosity, enough for her to turn to the title page where she notices the signature. She's the first to do so. She takes me upstairs at once, shows me surreptitiously to her companion; he promptly nods, pats her on the back, and pays for me, along with several other items. He produces a card, I notice, and asks for a 10 per cent discount. My heart sinks: another dealer! Is there no one out there who wants me for myself alone, and not for vile commercial purposes?

I am right, of course: he is far too pleased with himself to be anything else. Within an hour of having arrived at one second-hand bookshop, I'm being transported to another. As I go in I notice a sign saying 'Orbit Books', only a chap is busy at work removing graffiti from it, someone has sprayed in an 'ex' at the beginning and an 'ant' at the end. My price is rubbed out yet again (I'm getting a sore spot on the top right-hand corner of my front endpaper—I could kill for an osteopath). According to this man's calculations, I'm now worth all of £12. Something good's come out of it then, for I concede I felt cheap and nasty at 50p, still a bit grubby at £3, but here I've got some status in the world. Now at last, I'm thinking, someone who's read and enjoyed me, and fully appreciates the inscription, will buy me for my literary merit; indeed at £12, if anything, I'm a little worried that I've been priced beyond desirability. So now I'm standing on this shelf of signed hardbacks, rubbing shoulders with real nobs too—some of my companions are marked at £50 or more, and if I am not mistaken, look down on me, a mere paperback, as being too easy, too available, an upstart, *nouveau riche* little tart. I resent this, fruit yes, but tart... some of us have standards to keep up. In fact, I'm beginning to feel extremely uncomfortable in this élitist environment, and wondering if I'll ever get out of here. After all, will anyone pay £12 for a paperback, even if it is signed?

Clearly, despite my experiences, I am still an innocent, I should have been christened *Candide* and not 'Oranges', for this lady practically sidles up to me, lifts me off the shelf, checks my date of birth, closes her eyes in the most mysterious manner, and then (and only then) turns to the first page, her eyes darting open at the price. Her pupils widen, I notice, she emits an uncontrollable snort. What's her problem, I'm thinking, is she laughing at the price? Cow! No, horse, she's equestrianly English, massive too, she must be eighteen hands. So I'm only a paperback, that's no cause for her to start laughing at me. As I say, I'm still naïve, for hardly have I thought this than she strides up to the counter, slams me down on it (ouch!) and says 'this one please', and no, please God no, 'the usual 10 per cent, of course,' she adds.

Can you believe it?

When I've recovered from the shock, I observe that Exorbitant is in an even worse state than me. (As I said before, I can read too, sixty thoughts a minute.) His colour alone makes him legible, for he has turned a pale green, he knows now he is not as clever as he thought, he has made a mistake, and is visibly racking his brains to solve the mystery. Surely he couldn't have put more on a signed paperback? And to think that only three hours ago (yes, it is still the same day!) he was so pleased with himself. It's one thing to make a profit out of someone else's error, but to have the same thing done to him is twice as painful as the initial pleasure. And judging by the breadth of the grin on the lady's face, the error is a huge one. Exorbitant knows her well, she is a partner of the most exclusive first-edition firm in England, none other than the notorious Ava Rice (as I see from her cheque-book). Mr Singh and Mr Banerjee used to joke about being members of the Vauxhall Conference, worlds away from the premiership of Ava Rice and the like. Well, why would she bother with a signed paperback? Surely such an item wouldn't fit in with the rest of her stock? No, it's no use, he must reveal his ignorance, he simply has to find out. If only for next time. And he knows, life being the botch that it is—I refuse to say 'bitch'—there won't *be* a next time, which rubs salt into the wound.

'I presume there's an angle here. I mean, it is only a paperback.'

'But my dear Orbit, the first edition *was* a paperback.'

He looks at her dumbfounded. Bad enough to be called

exorbitant; even worse to suffer such abuse, and then fail to live up to it. Exorbitant—he? Charging £12 for a signed first edition of a trendy author's first novel? Perhaps he is thinking that next time he'll deface his own sign: how about Cheap and Cheerful Books instead? Before I'm packed away—he must still be reeling, for he's automaton-slow—I watch him moving his lips silently, as if calculating the figure that Ava Rice will now put on me. I can see this all the more in that I'm trying to calculate it myself. And I had never realised I was so important: it's quite a shock to my system. You see, as a paperback cloned into thousands, I never stopped to think which *edition* I was. Just think how I could have answered the insults of those toffee-nosed hardbacks.

I'm in awe as I enter the galleried wonder that is Ava Rice's establishment. A long room on two levels crammed with desks, a computer at each, a person at each computer, e-mails, faxes, the phone constantly ringing, even a few customers—and everywhere books, many of them sold, being put into parcels for the post office. She waves me in the air as she greets her colleagues, and while her manicured nails tap on my front cover, there is a general consultation, various three-figure sums are bandied back and forth. It makes me blush all the way down to my fore-edge. Eventually they agree, the now paltry-seeming figure of £12 is rubbed out, and the grand total of £350 is pencilled in instead. £350! I've *arrived*. Now surely, I'm thinking, this is it. I've even joined the ranks of the cabinet. I may be only a junior member, but in I go nevertheless, with various other gay or underground classics, some of them considerably hard to get, unhappy at having been stalked to their lair and plundered for profit. I ignore their tears: I mean, what's the point in getting your pages in a twist? Some of them are so extreme in their contents they look on me as positively square—but then, strictly speaking, we're all that, or at least rectangular. No dealer can buy me now, I'm truly a collector's item, though I confess I feel tired—it's been quite a day's travelling—as well as claustrophobic: it's rather airless under lock and key, we're all considerably relieved when it's opened up, and a customer has a browse inside.

THE JOURNEY OF THE BOOK

Books come and go from the cabinet, I make new friends and then lose them again, till, two weeks later, a huge imposing man in a wide-brimmed hat asks me to be fished out. He looks me up and down, fondles me all over in no uncertain terms (and I can tell you, though I don't have feet, my bottom edge is very ticklish), and having checked out my condition, grunts, paying the full £350 without any fuss. Phew! No discount this time, he's not a dealer but a person, a reader, thank God!

The name on the credit card reads Esmond Thete—I soon learn that he's Es to his friends—and before I know where I am I'm sitting in a taxi, going up in a lift in a Mayfair hotel, packed up in a heavy suitcase, locked in the boot of a car, sliding down a chute at the airport, and flying for the first time, winging my way across the Atlantic. True, I'm a little sad at leaving behind my native shelves, and so disoriented by the jet lag I don't know my first chapter from my last. But when I see my new home, a plush apartment on New York's Upper East Side, and when I find myself standing on a rosewood shelf in close proximity with five thousand other expensive first editions, I'm not complaining. All these wonderful books—what a shame I can't read them!—maybe they've all been on a similar journey to mine, from shop to shop, from reader to reader, acquiring value along the way, because their authors became fashionable, won prizes, or caused a scandal.

Most of these books have taken a circuitous route, have been culled from every corner of the globe, but all roads, it seems, lead to Es Thete, one of the world-renowned collectors, a connoisseur of modern literature with a catholic taste and a fastidious eye for condition. (So fitting, too, that his money should come from the family business—timber!) Of course, he never reads his books, oh no, not one of us, if I thought I would be appreciated again as by my first owner I was mistaken. No, old Es reads only library copies, and he treats these any old how, bending back the hinges until the book practically splits, spilling coffee on them, tossing them onto the floor when he's finished. *We*, on the other hand, inhabit an inner sanctum, a private shrine where no drinks are allowed, no smoke circulates, the room is kept at an even temperature.

THE JOURNEY OF THE BOOK

Naturally we're also curtained off from direct sunlight—you know, we tan very easily. He comes in several times a day and admires us, occasionally he risks picking one of us up, inhaling our body odour, but a sniff or a touch is all he allows himself, we are soon replaced. But even if I'm not read, as a book ought to be, I realise that's because I'm no longer a book but a fetish, an object of worship.

And so I eke out the days, months, years, but as I'm not overexerted physically, I don't age much; nor, because I keep cool, do I expand, I've still got a decent shape. Some of my pages are slightly foxed, it is true, but not as badly as my owner's hands. It is Es who grows older and vaster and crankier, he gets about less and less, his purchases slow down, he becomes a virtual recluse. Until one day, quite unexpectedly, he bends down to the bottom shelf where I happen to live, picks me out, is about to straighten himself up, when suddenly he cries out, puts me back at an angle, staggers violently, and falls with his whole galumphing weight on top of me and my neighbours at the base of the column. And I thought it was shelves that collapsed on people!

Well, it was a good life while it lasted, I can't really complain, I know of many books that remain completely neglected, at least I've travelled a bit, I've been lucky on the whole to have people who looked after me. Of course, as I lie here dying, I can't help feeling a little sorry for myself, didn't someone once say that each man kills the thing he loves, well, Es, it seems, has done for me, what with my spine being broken, my contents loosened by his awesome weight. It is some days before his body is discovered by a curious neighbour, and by then Es and Oranges and all the other books adjacent to me are lying in a pool of blood, from where he cut his head open on the edge of the wood. Strictly blood oranges now, my juice is running, my days as a collector's item are over, simultaneous with the collector himself.

And now his niece comes in to look after his children, the vast collection is valued by an auctioneer, thousands of books are packed up, row after row of rarities acquired with the dedication and perseverance of a lifetime. Each and every one of them worth a small fortune in itself, now to be sold on again, singly, or in small batches, to be picked off at auction by other collectors, dealers, institutes. All these books that had converged from the four corners of the earth into one private library, divergent once more, sucked back into the commercial maelstrom, sent backwards and forwards like tennis balls, temporary, like their owners, until age or accident finally does for them, and they are ready for the shredder.

Like me. There were sixteen casualties when Es had his fatal heart attack, sorry, seventeen if I include Es himself. I must remember that people are important too. But must I? Why remember anything now, as I lie mangled in a PVC bag (yes, one of those again) in the dustbin outside, along with several of my comrades, waiting for the garbage truck to take me away. Oh God, has it come to this, I who have passed through so many hands and ended up in a famous library, to be reduced to a bloody pulp in a sack.

What was that? There's no mistaking that noise, the grinding and churning of the garbage truck turning into our street, stopping outside each house, and now I hear the tell-tale squeak of our area gate being opened, heavy steps approach, I brace myself as I am swung onto somebody's shoulder, my pages start to flutter with fear. I, Oranges, a rotting fruit, one that has slipped up on the banana skin of life, a life in the end as bitter as a lemon, am tossed into the air, one moment printed matter (I'm not looking forward to this) and the next (I'm not—

10

Auctions

Auctions are more competitive than they've ever been. There are more dealers about, it seems, not just every year, but every week. With the spread of local book fairs, the popularity of periodicals like *The Book and Magazine Collector*, the increase in early retirement and second careers, it's not surprising that everybody's at it, every other person one meets 'knows a thing or two about books'. And a few of them really do. So how do I ever buy anything? The simple answer is, I don't much; I know a little about everything, but I'm not an expert in any one area, I haven't cornered a particular market. The *haute cuisine* falls to the specialists; I tend to scavenge on the left-overs. Whether it be bibles, Baedekers, plate books or whatever, these specialists have acquired a vast stock in their field, and go out of their way to supplement it, often paying well over the odds to ensure no one else gets a look-in. This is how they maintain their stranglehold. But no one is really secure. Not only can another dealer come along (someone with sufficient capital to back him up) and decide that this is his preferred area too, but there is competition from foreign dealers coming over for the big auctions, even, on occasion, the challenge of private collectors. I presume it is 'on occasion' and not more widespread, or book dealers, who work on a certain percentage, would not be able to compete. If the going price for a book is £2,000, and a collector knows that and is willing to pay it, clearly he is in a stronger position than a dealer, who will pay half, maybe even three-quarters if he has a particular client in mind, but not more. Wouldn't it be amusing if the specialist, perched oh-so-complacently in his chair in the auction room, suddenly found himself bidding against his own customer, who returned his jerk-forward shock of recognition with a knowing wink and a wave?

If, if, if ... Auctions are nothing if not a gamble: the winning bidder, the underbidder (offering the second highest price) and the also-rans are as unpredictable as racehorses. Sometimes the favourite romps home; sometimes it is a comparatively dark horse, an outsider, who snatches it. My experience of auctions is a peculiar one: while I have viewed and left bids at many venues, so pressed am I for time that I am rarely able to attend one. So if I do make a successful bid, or if I miss by inches or by miles, I'm not in a position to find out why. Some auction houses tell you the name of the successful bidder, from which one can make a general hypothesis; others do not. But no amount of information can tell you why a lot that you thought was worth £400 sells for £2,500. Somewhere you've made a huge miscalculation: you may have forgotten some issue point about the rarer grey variant of a normally green cloth; or that pamphlet you didn't check that was facing the wrong way was doing so for a very good reason; or an author's name you didn't recognise was actually the pseudonym of someone very famous indeed.

It is not likely to be the buyer's mistake, because at least one contender has bid him up to that amount. And while there is plenty of rivalry and mutual dislike in the book trade, it is pushing it to suppose that one dealer will risk running another up to a ridiculously high figure just out of malice; after all, he doesn't want to be landed with the bill himself. Of course, there is another motive for trying to secure a higher price at someone else's expense—the lot could be yours. As far as I know, it is perfectly legal to get the ball rolling by bidding on your own books. I have not heard of a case of a dealer falling victim to his own game, whipping up a frenzy only to realise that everyone else has suddenly dropped out, and the lot is his. But it must have happened. The look on his face when he has to fork out £200 for a pile of junk he couldn't wait to get off his hands!

Certainly people have been known to buy the wrong lot, even if it isn't their own: it might be something misheard down the phone (lot 50 instead of lot 15), or a jumbling up of lot and bid:

AUCTIONS

instead of leaving £180 on lot 620, you leave £620 on lot 180, and if the latter is worth only £100 you're in trouble. Worse still, you might fall asleep at an auction and wake up to what sounds like number 228, win the lot with ease, only to hear the gavel come down on lot 328 (down on your head, that is), for it is not the tree-calf Shelley you supposed, but a bunch of odd volume bindings in dire condition, sold, you notice, 'not subject to return'. A heart-fluttering phrase, that: when a bookseller reads this, he knows the lot is a stinker, that half if not all the books are defective, covers detached, pages missing, damp-stained, worm-holed, crumbling in your hands. Why anyone buys such a lot I don't know, but some people do—I mean, deliberately. In the usual run of things, if you find a book is defective, and it hasn't been catalogued as such, you have a short period of time in which to give it back. But 'not subject to return' means no matter what dreadful things you discover (the books were recently exhumed from a vault containing human remains from the plague), these babes are yours, and yours alone.

Some auction catalogues are scrupulously exact in their description of items for sale. If 'not subject to return' can be translated as 'suitable only for those of a suicidal disposition', other terms are less euphemistic: 'rubbed', 'faded', 'cocked', 'soiled', 'disbound', 'mispaginated', 'upside down', 'torn map', 'paper flaw', 'one plate xeroxed', 'half title missing'. With such prior warning in mind, a book will rarely appear worse on a shelf than it is described—often it will seem rather better, so anxious is the cataloguer not to mislead the potential bidder. Others are not quite so honest, or at least so painstaking in their verification of details: dates and editions wrongly given; 'slight rubbing at extremities' turning out to be pieces coming away; 'some fading to front cover' materialising as a once-verdant green bleached by the sun beyond all recognition; and 'a group of modern first editions in dust-jackets all in good condition'— absolutely fine, till you discover they're all stamped with 'Scunthorpe Polytechnic' inside. The reliability of collation and breadth of bibliographical knowledge will vary wildly from catalogue to catalogue. Only personal experience of each auction house will help you determine beforehand whether something is being described accurately, and is worth taking a trip to see.

Setting out for the auction, whether in London, the provinces or indeed abroad, is one thing: getting to see the books is another. As I say, there are so many dealers nowadays that the chances are, when you get there, someone is halfway through the particular lot you've come to see. Or if you do get a free run at a book, one dealer backs into you ('Oh, I'm sorry'), another reaches a hand right across your field of vision ('If I can just...'), while a third is rifling through a carton at your feet ('Excuse me but you're in my light'). Oh it's all very gentlemanly on the surface, there are no professional fouls, but in the jungle of the stacks these dealers are always whirring about you, they're as pestilential as mosquitoes.

I talked earlier about bibliophobes, an easy enough coinage for those with a horror of books; but there is no obvious word to hand for a person who has such a reaction to dealers. There should be: it is a common enough complaint, especially among those in the trade itself. Well, here goes. Juxtapose the words for book ('biblion') and man ('anthropos') and you arrive at 'anbibliothrope' (or 'book-man'); add a touch of hatred, with the prefix 'mis-', and you get, instead of 'misanthrope', that general enemy of mankind, the more specific 'misanbibliothrope' (or 'hater of book-men'). I am one of them, but alas there is no cure, for a book-man, if he wants to remain liquid, must inhabit the same territory as other (even slimier) book-men, i.e. auction rooms.

You may have noticed I'm being a shade 'whimsical' here, you may protest and say that booksellers are people, good and bad, I'm not being fair, who am I, another book-man after all, to bad-mouth everyone? Reader, as so often, you are right, and I apologise: book-men are human too. Prick a book-man, will he not bleed? Does not a book-man have eyes, nose, wallet, all the usual human accoutrements? Of course. (In fact, having seen two of them in a punch-up once, I can definitely say that they do bleed.) But though they have such attributes, when they are in an auction room, they revert to their status as book-men only, their humanity is all but dissipated. As for the supposition that I too am one of them, how can you be so wide of the mark? *I* am a lover of books who, it just so happens, dabbles in them as well; *they* are the enemy, traffickers, mere money-making book-men.

Yes, viewing books can be a frustrating experience, and not simply because of such obstruction. Next there is the problem of finding the lots you've marked in advance for special attention. These come in all shapes and sizes, single books, a group of five, or a 'quantity' lot (often as many as 200), and they are arranged as much according to spatial convenience as they are in strict numerical order. (A member of staff will normally have a plan, and be able to assist you.) Then there is the problem of the books themselves. If, like me, you work in a large general bookshop, you are looking for reasonable quantity lots as well as singles or small groups. These are very hard to find. Often a library is broken up in such a way by the cataloguer that all the large lots tend to be a mixture of good, solid saleable stock and out-and-out stinkers. It is a consistent annoyance to come across, say, three large lots of some hundred books each, find twenty in this one that you want, ten in that, and just a single itsy-bitsy item from the third (the rest you want to annihilate). I'm sure all booksellers have played this game of mental rearrangement. Of course, the cataloguer knows exactly what he's doing: he's putting the bad in with the good so as to move it on; if he put all the good together, and all the bad, he'd lose out: the better lots would fetch more, certainly, but the rubbish wouldn't sell at all. I said it was a mental indulgence, but one hears rumours of booksellers moving books *physically* from one lot to another. Now I can understand this, and it's all very creative (here's one I prepared earlier), but unfortunately it's also illegal. No, our role is to suffer the eternal curate's egg of the large lot—a free range, and so full of shit. We also have to suffer (in certain auction houses that will not be mentioned) on our hands and knees. General lots are often arranged in cubby-holes at the bottom of the stacks, and we must face the humiliation of scrabbling about on all fours, fetching piles of books out from within the darkness, checking them over, then putting them back as neatly as we can.

But this is not the end of the frustration (I've barely started).

AUCTIONS

Sometimes I'm a third the way through a large quantity of books, they've been quite promising to begin with, then they start to deteriorate rapidly, and it dawns on me that this is not only the usual good-and-bad mix but something far worse—a dealer's lot. Yes, we're back to those book-men again: one of this wretched breed has decided to sell off his dross, in the hope that some schmuck like me will come along and be fooled. All right, I'll come clean, I've been a dupe more than once, I suspect we all have, particularly in our tyro auction viewing days. But not any more. No, now I'm more likely to do it myself—cook up a load of junk I can't sell, stir with a few rather better ingredients, and then garnish with a maraschino of a book to whet the appetite of the unsuspecting buyer.

This heinous habit can have variable results. It seems that whenever anyone else indulges, it's a culinary success, the lot fetches a respectable figure; but whenever I do it my fingers get burnt, it fetches as little as it deserves, or is even 'bought in'. This is the auctioneer's term for any lot that fails to meet the reserve—the minimum price the seller is prepared to accept—or, in the case of no reserve being left (as here), fails to elicit so much as a single bid. The result: I am penalised for wasting their time, *and* I have to take my books away again. Maybe there is a certain art to this disguise, and I haven't mastered it yet: am I really so hopeless at deceit, so doomed to honesty?

In fact, trade lots can be notorious for their trickery. These book-men don't just stop at attractive books as bait; they have a whole array of practical jokes up their sleeves. How about putting in a first edition, for instance, except that if you look closely enough, the line underneath, the one that should read 'second impression' or 'colonial edition', has been Tipp-Exed out. Let's try a faked signature while we're about it, someone relatively minor perhaps whose handwriting is not too well known (and someone not too dead either at the time the book was printed!). And why stop at signatures? There have occasionally been letters, simulacra too, secreted towards the rear of a book maybe, but liable to tumble out if you give it a good flick. And then our old favourite, the pencil price that has been rubbed out, oh quite thoroughly, but not, you are bound to notice, quite thoroughly enough—£50 it says, when it has a face value of £10. This is puerile, amateurish stuff you'll say, and naturally the experienced dealer will be chortling away at this juncture. But you never know who's going to view this auction, someone new to the trade perhaps, or some poor innocent who's strayed in off the street and knows nothing of the lures and traps of the anbibliothrope.

The next frustration is, even if you've decided there are enough good books in the lot to balance the bad ones, and you haven't put your back out in the process, what bid do you leave on it? You glance at the estimate (£100–£150), which is often pitched considerably below the price the lot will realise (a psychological ploy to raise your hopes and encourage you to bid), and make sure your offer's at least within this range. Excluding all the dross you don't want, you calculate £750 as the total resale value of the books—the big question is, how much do you rate them? For a really good consistent lot I'm prepared to pay half, which takes me up to £375. But I have to pay 15 per cent premium to the auction house on top of this, so I must now subtract 15 per cent of £375, approximately £55, which takes me back down to £320. Then I have to consider what a rival dealer is thinking, will his calculations be the same as mine? In that case, I'll go up one bid to £330, in order to clinch it. The trouble is, my rival may be thinking ditto, so I even consider raising the stakes to £340. But this kind of oneupmanship could go on ad infinitum, and now I find myself reversing, no, £320 was right in the first place, too bad if it goes for more. And what happens? It goes for £330, and I'm not saying 'too bad', I'm cursing. Bloody hell! But it's more than likely that whatever I had left it would have gone for one bid more.

Coming second is the most frustrating thing of all, but at least it means you know your stuff, you've learned something in your x number of years, you can take some comfort from that. Oh yes. If only I was as good at deceiving others as I seem to be ... No, there's nothing so comforting as success, even if you have to pay up to the hilt for it. However, I don't wish to sound too negative; one isn't always the underbidder at auction. Oh no: sometimes one's way out! As I said earlier, I can leave £400 on a lot, and it goes for £2,500. Whoops! Or, inexplicably, I can leave £500 on a lot I expect to be fiercely contested, and get it for £200. I suppose everybody has their turn—to believe in a benevolent God, that is; well, here's mine.

It happened to me recently at an auction of music books. There were small lots focusing on particular composers: several books on Haydn, including the massive Robbins-Landon biography; a select group of Brahmsiana; the Second Viennese School all roped together, and many, many more. Two hours later, when I thought I'd viewed all the possibilities, I noticed a quantity lot on Wagner just sitting in a cubby-hole, virgin, untouched. I assumed either there was something wrong with them, or their tidy state was misleading, and they'd been thoroughly investigated after all. I suspect some dealers put the books back neatly as a devious ploy: it creates the impression that nobody has looked at the lot, in which case it's not worth you looking at it either, or a low bid should at least be enough to clinch it. There again, this could just be my deviousness. Whatever the truth, I decided to have a go. I began on the first pile, waded in a little deeper, and soon realised I was just too tired to proceed any further—what if I were to fall asleep, and curl up at the back of the cupboard? The victorious bidder might bag me up with the rest of the books, a cumbersome elephant folio, I might end up on a similar journey to Oranges.

But seriously, I saw enough to know it was the best lot in the auction. Every aspect of Wagner was covered: early publications of his own writings, volumes of correspondence, several 'definitive' biographies, numerous studies of *The Ring*, scholarly dissertations on Bayreuth, anti-Semitism and proto-Nazi propaganda. Surely everyone had seen it, and it would reach some astronomical price. I left a half-hearted bid of £500, based on the small percentage I'd been patient enough to examine. In other words I guessed, and as always was cautious in my guessing. When I phoned up for the results I encountered the usual litany of nowhere-nears and almost-but-not-quites. Haydn danced jauntily to a tune beyond my means; Brahms roared down at me from a distant peak; while Schoenberg and his cronies cackled out some cacophonous figure. When I came to my final bid, the Wagner, I expected this leitmotiv to continue, the price to soar into the regions of Valhalla.

I braced myself accordingly.

'Lot 217?'
'Let me see now.' A rustle of papers. '200.'
'I'm sorry?'
'200, sir.'
'But... who...?'
'Why you, sir. You of course.'

For there's always the possibility of some mix-up: the bid you faxed them was either illegible or simply omitted by mistake. Being me, I was sceptical all the way up to the time for collection. No, they really were mine, and as I packed them up, bringing out from behind the books that had been obscured from view, I discovered more and more of the same quality. And in good condition too. If it didn't add up to a vast amount of money, it was a steal nonetheless. Inexplicable. I can only suppose the lot was missed. It wasn't in an obscure corner, or in a separate room, as can happen; the music dealers had looked high and low (the other lots went for well above the estimates), but had somehow managed to overlook it. Maybe they're an especially lazy bunch, and can't face rummaging *adagio* through a cubby-hole; maybe they're all Jewish. And yet it's amazing how energetic, how unprejudiced people can become when money is involved.

Alas, this sort of fortune is unusual. In fact, even when successful at securing large lots at auction, yet further frustrations are possible. For one thing, it's easy enough writing out a bid of £500 on a slip of paper; it's almost as easy to write out a cheque (especially when it's the firm's money, not mine). What's not so easy is packing them up. When I think of two hundred hardback books, I think merely of twenty bags of ten books each; but if the thought is compact and expeditious enough, the action is less so. It's not just the repetitive strain of lifting them up, over and over again, into the bags, I then have to lift the bags out of the auction room into a taxi, out of the taxi into the shop, and then down the stairs into the stock room. Quite often, too, two hundred books, even when not part of a trade lot, but a private collection, will have been purchased originally at second hand; i.e. they have two hundred pencilled-in prices to be rubbed out, one by one, and then re-priced. (This is particularly galling if the wrong pencil has been used, leaving an indelible mark.)

Another frustration is that books glanced at necessarily in a hurry in an auction room can look very different in a new environment. Viewing them, one was assessing them on their merits over and against other lots of inferior ones. Removed from that venue, and now isolated, they can look pretty ordinary too. I'm not the only bookseller who has got his hard-won booty back in the shop and asked himself: 'Why on earth did I buy these?' The light can play tricks on you as well. In the rather dull light of the auction room (even duller near the floor where the general lots so often are) the books take on a uniform brightness of colour; back in the brightly lit shop they can look correspondingly dull. It's as if they've gone through some metamorphosis. It could be more serious still: one book, on close examination, actually *is* in a worse state than when you viewed it: some bookman has put a dirty paw-print on it and nicked the dust-jacket. Or the best book isn't even there: either a genuine mistake has been made, and your prize item has strayed into an adjacent lot; or, more likely, someone has fallen victim to that temptation I mentioned earlier.

So why go to auctions at all? Because booksellers always need fresh stock to liven up their establishments, and that is one way of acquiring it; because you can be lucky, or your cunning can pay off, and it is satisfying to outwit the opposition; above all, when you phone up for the results you get the same buzz that a gambler gets when he turns to the sports column in the morning and looks at the 1-2-3 for the 4.15 at Haydock. If your calculations have been correct, a successful bid means time well spent, a job well done, and last but not least, a tidy profit. If you get nothing, you say to yourself you'll never bother again, but this feeling soon wears off, just as the more a gambler loses the more he's determined to have another go and lose some more. Of course, if you know what you're doing, the only thing you lose at auction is time and effort, though this can be considerable. And as for that underbidder business ... More often than not, I suspect, I lose out to someone who has driven there specially to attend, and is intent on taking something away with him, if only to pay for the petrol. He may even bid several notches above his maximum to get it. (And if he has landed another lot well under the bid earlier, this gives him a practical advantage: he has more room to manoeuvre, more money to play with.) Being an absentee bidder puts me in a weaker position then; I should try to attend more often, take each result as it comes, and adjust my bids accordingly.

Even so, it's a fairly mind-numbing business. Anyone expecting a roll-up, roll-up atmosphere is in for a disappointment; it's grey and drab, and has as much in common with a funeral as a circus. In a subdued, monotonous voice the auctioneer goes through the lots in the catalogue, often as many as 120 or 150 per hour. He starts somewhere beneath the estimate, and winds it up without too much fuss when the last rival bidder drops out. The only variation is in who's doing the bidding. Sometimes it is the auctioneer (representing the absentee bidder) versus someone in the room; or it is two people present vying with each other until one drops out (though a third, having let the other two do all the donkey work, may snatch it at the end with a late flurry of interest); or it's a battle between two anonymous individuals, ie. an absentee bidder against a person on the phone, calling from somewhere in England or possibly overseas. The professional auctioneer shows very little interest in the proceedings; to him it's all business as usual. He does not get excited when relatively large amounts are being banded about, nor does he sound too deflated when the bidding fails to reach the estimate. He simply mutters to his assistant: 'Lot unsold'. There can be a surprising number of these, due either to the excessive optimism of the valuer, or the greed of the seller who may have disregarded his advice.

AUCTIONS

The atmosphere at contemporary auctions (I can't speak for the past) is utterly informal. Bidders do not have to sit still; they often move around at will, spot someone they know coming in, and walk across the room to have a chat. Knowing book-men, this is probably book-talk; whether it goes as far as conspiracy is another matter. You may have heard of 'the ring' (and no, I'm not going to bore you with any more Wagner stories). This is the term used for a group of dealers who agree between themselves just who is to get which lot, withholding their bids where appropriate, so that items are knocked down to each comparatively cheaply. This procedure was rife in the old days, where it amounted almost to organised crime; I suspect there are just too many interlopers for it to work more than patchily nowadays. You'd be hard put to suss out anything dodgy going on. Book-men sit slumped in any old position, on chairs, on the floor, on the dais below the bookshelves with their backs to the wall, laughing, snoozing, reading a newspaper, as they wait for the relevant lot to come up. There is very little drama, though it is quite possible to be distracted at the crucial moment by the constant chatter of voices going on around you, even for your view of the auctioneer to be blocked by some dealer crossing the floor.

I have to admit to a certain nervousness in the auction room. Sometimes I'm convinced that I've caught the auctioneer's eye, and that he's pointing at me with his finger of fate, while announcing 'Ah, a new bidder, two thousand five hundred'. My heart's practically in my mouth before I discover that a chap in front of me has taken up the bidding (though I'm damned if I saw him shift an inch) and won the lot. Bidders do it very discreetly; they either raise their paddle (a wooden stick with a reference number on it to identify you), or lift their pen, or nod almost imperceptibly. Then they keep nodding until a shake of the head indicates that they have bowed out. And yet it must happen: someone tries to suppress a sneeze and nods at the wrong moment, or reaches his hand up to scratch behind his shirt collar, and finds himself committed to spending a fortune on a book he's never even heard of.

AUCTIONS

'Sold for five thousand to the man on the aisle there.'
'But you don't understand—I've got eczema.'
'I'm sorry, sir, that hardly exempts you from payment.'

It would be difficult to find the time to protest, the auctioneer is so keen to move on to the next lot, and does so with all speed, perhaps as much for this reason as to get through his lengthy agenda. Thousands of pounds change hands in a matter of seconds. The auctioneer runs it up, first in tens, 50, 60, then twenties and thirties, 200, 220, 250, then fifties, 500, 550, then hundreds, 1,000, 1,100, so that you have to think and above all react with razor-sharp timing. He conducts this mini-ensemble with his head, which swivels back and forth like a baton. And he keeps up this regular tempo for several hours: lot 24, a set of Byron... lot 156, a batch of Chartist pamphlets... lot 291, *Extraordinary Popular Delusions and the Madness of Crowds*.

The hysteria of the last-named would be impossible here: the whole world outside might have been informed of imminent apocalypse, and the auctioneer would doubtless still be droning on in his practised level voice. Talk about 'unsold': try and sell *him* the idea that the world has come to an end.

'Sir, sir,' the receptionist rushes in, 'there's a rumour going round that we're all doomed.'
'What *are* you talking about?'
'The Day of Judgment, sir, it's arrived.'
'My dear chap, even if the Beaujolais Nouveau has arrived, I don't wish to be disturbed.'
'But it's true.'
'Don't be tiresome.' (Turning back to the room.) 'Now what am I bid for this fine edition of Nostradamus, how about 300, 320, and is that 350 on the phone there?'
'No,' says the assistant manning one of the outside lines, 'it's official confirmation.'
'Confirmation?'
'From God.'

'Now how on earth did he get on the line?'
'The reception's dreadful. As for the news...'
'What does he say?'
'"Going, going, gone".'
'Plagiarist! Would you kindly tell him not to interrupt? Unless, of course, he'd like to leave a bid; no, on second thoughts, he's probably got a copy. Now where was I? 320 was it, yes, do I hear 350, thank you sir, 380...?'

It is such a thing as the sheer relentlessness of this series of figures, the utter blandness of the auction room, a kind of world in microcosm, that convinces me it'll never come to an end. Quite frankly, who, or what, would expend the effort to terminate something so trivial, so absurd?

11

Private Libraries

Not everyone chooses to sell their books this way. Some people are put off by the delay (up to six months before they come up), the commission (20 per cent of the hammer price goes to the auction house), and by the uncertainty of the result. While many do well, even, occasionally, beyond their wildest dreams, others are disappointed. Whoever put in that Wagner lot, for instance, must have expected more. Auctions are a gamble: they offer no guarantee that the right figure will be reached. While freakishly high prices can be obtained (the result perhaps of two private collectors determined on one particular item and prepared to go to inordinate lengths to get it), others are unaccountably low. It may be that a lot looks so sexy, so obviously expensive, that the more fatalistic dealers don't even bother to bid, and if enough of them have the same attitude...

The best alternative to auctioning off your collection is to call booksellers in to make an offer. This method has several advantages: it cuts out any delay, there is no deductible commission, and you know exactly how much money the books will fetch before reaching a final decision. Of course, many people turn this into a private auction: they call in numerous dealers, one after another, and sell to the highest bidder. But it's not the same. The books will not be viewed by as great a gathering of dealers from all over the country; and the possibility of private buyers is ruled out. Nor do these sellers tend to portion out their books into categories and ask for separate offers; they usually want an overall price. Now when you view ten books at an auction, or even a hundred, your concentration is reasonably steady; but if you're looking at several hundred, or thousand, you start to get lazy, you can't be bothered to value every single one. After a while, you find yourself taking an average of books per shelf at such-and-such a price, and because of the work anticipated in clearing such a library, it's a pretty conservative estimate at that. You end up bidding rather less conscientiously than you might on a more select number of books.

So in both cases the seller will lose out: by paying commission in one quarter, and by sheer quantity in another. Actually even if you opt for the auction method, the more prestigious firms will come and pick out only what they want anyway; you'll still have the bulk of books on your hands to dispose of. Unless you open your own shop, and sell off your library piecemeal to the general public, there's not much in it for you. The fact is, good books are at a premium, they're wanted by everybody and are easy to sell; but the vast majority (to a bookseller's eye at least) are ordinary, and these count for little. A lot of people do not understand this. They equate quantity with quality ('How can you give me £200 for one book, and £10 for fifty?'), or, more frequently, they imagine that the books that mean most to them—whether for literary or sentimental reasons—will have the same appeal for others. It cannot be said too often that a well-written book may have no commercial value, and a book that fetches money may be... well...

Take *The Naked Lunch*, for instance. Fans of this novel would doubtless argue that it puts the beat back into beatitude; for others, it is the degraded, formless, scatological ravings of a gun-toting, wife-killing, low-life junkie scumbag. You detect a personal note? Actually I'm sitting on the fence; I prefer to keep a critical distance in these matters. Which is why I've just chucked it into the neighbour's garden: far and away—I can say it now—this is the worst book I've ever read.

In principle I like the idea of house calls; there's something rather exciting about the prospect of entering unknown territory. I have to say it's not all velvet armchairs, silver tea services and mahogany sideboards; sometimes it's a sleazy bedsit or a house in a state of terminal neglect. But whether rich or poor, it's an adventure; you always hope that this is the one, the treasure trove you've been waiting for, and even though time after time you are disappointed, hope springs eternal in the human sole. Don't shout at the proofreader: I mean, I'm positively light-footed as I approach the front door and then follow the occupant up the stairs.

Then I see the books.

'Er... didn't you say something about two hundred bindings?'
'Yes. What's the problem?'
'Well... how shall I put this?... there aren't any.'
'So what do you call these?'
'A travesty. In a word, Heron books.'
'They're bound, aren't they?'
'No, madam, they are not bound. In fact, I am bound to say they're made of a tawdry pretend sort of leather that wouldn't fool anyone, with the apparent exception of your good self.'
'Well, I like that!'
'Then I'll continue. They are bound to attract people with a similarly artificial view of the world, one that's all surface glitz, without substance to back it up. You see, they are not bound for glory, but destined for those who don't really like books. I'm sorry, do you find that offensive?'
'Yes. And you're trying it on. Of course they're leather.'
'Madam, you put me in a bit of a bind; for I have to say there is only one thing in this room of a bovine consistency.'
'Out of my house!'
'With pleasure. Indeed I am homeward bound. Thank you for wasting my time.'

This is one of the many ways in which people can lure you in under false pretences. To be fair—if only for a moment—in nine cases out of ten, I suspect, it is not deliberate. It is sheer ignorance that makes people talk of a 'wide selection of literature' (which turns out to be *Reader's Digest* abridgements); of 'collectable' books (books on collecting, in fact); of 'foreign literature in translation' (Pirandello in Spanish, Cervantes in French, Balzac in Italian). Lisping doesn't help matters either—books on ethics sound fine, only you're halfway to Southend before it suddenly dawns on you ... It is because people have misled me so often in the past that I'm now inclined to put them through a Gestapo-style interrogation on the phone beforehand. More often than not, they're not so much misleading as infuriatingly vague.

'Hello. I hear you buy books.'
'That depends. What exactly do you have?'
'Oh, all kinds.'
'Could you be more specific?'
'It's difficult to say. It's a complete mish... mizzle... Something for everyone, you might say.'
'Are we talking history perhaps? Literature?'
'Oh yes.'
'Which?'
'Both. Come and have a look. It's a real mizzle... mish... mishellany.'
'The trouble is, you see, you live ten miles away; we like to have as clear an idea as possible before agreeing to view.'
'I quite understand.'
'Hmm. You said history, for instance...'
'Did I?'
'All right. *I* said history—'
'Well... strictly speaking... no, there isn't any.'
'There must be something concrete.'
'It's all... oh dear, how can I put it?... a bit of a—'
'Please! Don't say it. "Mixture" will do.'

Aaaaah!!!

At such times even Portnoy himself couldn't scream as loudly as your average put-upon bookseller. True enough, some of these libraries are being sold on another's behalf, but people are often as vague about their own books. How can you not know what you have? I mean, if you know what a book *is*, surely it's possible to describe it, or, failing that, read out the title?

Basically, I don't trust these people; they don't deserve to be visited. It's not only what they've got they're vague about; it's also how much. Unless they sound like rare books, I'm only prepared to come out and view them if there's a sufficient quantity.

'How many roughly?'
'Oh... loads.'
'Do you mean a hundred? A thousand?'
'Now you're asking. Dozens. Is that less than a hundred?'
'That all depends on how many dozens... *doesn't it?*'
'Don't you call me Dozen-tit!'
'Sorry?... Look. Let's try again. How many shelves?'
'I don't know. They're in the other room.'
'Could you go and count?'
'I'm telling you it's a reasonable amount.'
'Reasonable to whom?'
'You know, you ask an awful lot of questions.'

I do. I have to. How often have two thousand books turned out to be two hundred (some people are as innumerate as others are illiterate), or a wall turned out to be a shelf, or twenty boxes, well, twenty boxes, only *shoe* boxes, not boxes boxes. Occasionally people *under*-sell: they say they've got over a hundred books, and strictly speaking they have—a thousand, in fact. This can be almost as annoying. Because I don't drive I tend to travel partly on foot, weighed down with heavy carrier bags in case the deal is struck on the spot and the books are to go at once. If the quantity is considerably more than I bargained for, then I'm not fully prepared: it's a matter of going down to the local supermarket and scrounging for empty boxes. If it's considerably less, I've carried all those heavy bags for nothing. Which is why when I call, I want them to take the Bible in their right hand, and tell the truth, the whole truth and nothing but the truth; I want chapter and verse, preferably revelations. God spare me from any more bubble-headed daughters who wouldn't recognise a book title even if it summed them up perfectly—*Clueless*, *The Empty Space*; or some senile old man who can barely vouch for the fact that he's still alive, let alone tell me what he has for sale. I mean, there's a time for humanity, and tolerance, and compassion, but this isn't it. This is *business*.

Of course, the circumstances are often sad. Death is the commonest factor, and not only old people, but a lot of younger people too (many libraries have come out of the AIDS epidemic). Then again, it might be a couple splitting up, or moving to a smaller location; or an older person with a massive accumulation of books who must now go into a nursing home, or wants to travel round the world before leaving it altogether. What use are books in the end? You can't take them with you, and all the knowledge gleaned from them and life in general ultimately slips through our fingers into a permanent void. So is it wiser to be ignorant, unthinking, bookless, more honest too, for nothing is both our starting-point and our destination? I can't believe this. If our brains are to rot, why encourage them to do so prematurely, why not put off the evil day with a gesture of defiance—we may be deceiving ourselves, our grasp at knowledge may be futile, but it is *knowingly* futile. Keats called this fancy of ours 'a deceiving elf', and though this personification has always jarred with me (not least because of his flagrant need to rhyme *something* with 'self'), it is indeed mischievous, inhuman. For how can we forget that we are going to die? And yet I am quite convinced that even if we know we are, and very soon (like Keats), our instinct for survival will stay with us till the very last minute. If only in the most trivial details. One thinks of Orwell's essay *A Hanging*, for instance, in which a prisoner carefully sidesteps a puddle on the way to the gallows. And there'll be a hundred other examples one can think of, the majority—guess what—from books.

Another digression? Oh... all right then. I thought it was rather profound myself.

But whatever the reason for them being sold (it might even be a landlord flogging off those of a tenant who has scarpered overnight without paying his rent), one never knows quite what to expect. As I've already said, the books are usually less desirable than they are made to sound on the phone; but sometimes they are better. A man called me once and admitted straight away that a couple of specialists had already been through them, all he had left was fairly run-of-the-mill. It was all I could do to summon up the enthusiasm to go at all, but I liked his honesty (almost no one would confess to a previous sifting), it was lean times, and nothing ventured ... What did I find? Three hundred books, mostly of military history, recent certainly, and nothing rare, but all mint in their dust-jackets, scarcely read, and perfectly acceptable at £1 each, thank you very much. That was what he *asked* for. As far as he was concerned, what remained was merely a burden to him, he was happy to see the back of them. I was happy too; we were both very happy.

But before you send me your congratulations, let me tell you that such happiness is rare in these circumstances. I've seen grown men practically in tears when, for one reason or another, they've had to sell off their libraries. As soon as I arrive, the client takes me to the bookcase, indicates what's for sale (also what's not—*very* tantalising—I prefer not to see these at all), and then leaves me to it. This is not just so that I can concentrate better without someone breathing down my neck; they can't bear anyone so much as touching their books. And when the price is agreed, and it's time to bag them all up, they're nowhere to be found.

But this is not the only kind of unhappiness. Far more often, this is to do with money. Making an offer on a large library is very complex. It is not simply a question of the value of the books and the percentage I'm prepared to pay; as in an auction lot, it's to do with the proportion that I really want, and how quickly they will turn over. When it comes to private libraries there are two other crucial factors: what does the seller expect for the books, and is anyone else going to view them apart from me? Of course, one can't ask these questions directly; but it's possible to arrive at an answer by a roundabout method.

'You sound very young to have such a large library. Are these your books or...'

'They're an inheritance—from my father.'

Right. So this person is unlikely to know the books inside out, what each of them cost, which are the rarer items etc. etc. Another useful pointer is the following question:

'And if I make an offer, and it's acceptable, is it feasible to take the books today? If not, I don't want to carry heavy bags with me.'

'As a matter of fact I'm calling several dealers in after you, so...'

There I have it: now I know I have some competition. I don't always have the opportunity to determine so much beforehand; either people don't grasp what you're driving at, or they understand only too well. But it is true to say that if I know other dealers will be looking at the books, the price I offer is likely to be a little higher. If I really want the books, it will only make a slight difference, for I won't want to risk losing them by pitching too low. On the other hand, if the books are only so-so, and I know for a fact there is no competition, the person is not expecting a fortune, it may make a considerable difference. Obviously there is a diplomacy in buying and selling, and if the seller is not well versed in this, that's his lookout.

But I don't wish to give the wrong impression: if I've ever made a killing, it's not through me pulling the trigger; it's the seller who's turned the gun on himself. Some people are extraordinarily unworldly, and all but donate the books to you; failing that, they name a figure that can only be based on what they paid for the books decades before. Sometimes I take pity on them at this point, and buck it up, if only just a little. If you buck it up too much, they may become suspicious, confused, even unhappy, and you may do yourself out of business—fuck it up, in fact. This may sound sophistical, but it is also true; in the long run they'll be more satisfied if you offer them what they want. (If you offer them any lower—and this is standard procedure in most situations of this kind—you're a crack businessman, but you're also a swine, and I don't know how you can sleep at night.)

Another thing: it's possible to offer too little in all innocence. Scanning a large library, you get an overall impression of the wood, even some of the trees, but not every acorn. Often when you've brought the books back and are going through them, you find an unexpected treasure. That's when you realise you could have paid another hundred or two... all right, five. But if you didn't know the book was there, you can be pretty damn sure they didn't either (besides, someone who knows what he has will almost certainly point out the gems beforehand). I once bought a very dull collection for very little; I don't think most of the books were worth more than £5 each. Buried among this plethora of mediocrity, however, I later unearthed a slim, fragile, inconspicuous volume of verse called *Mount Zion*, signed as it happened by its author, a certain John Betjeman, and this was his first book. A piece of the backstrip was missing, it was by no means a perfect copy, but rare enough for that one item to have doubled the value of the whole collection. This is quite usual, and one of the rewards for the hard work of buying a large library: viewing, packing, lugging, pricing. And the profit has to be more than double, more than triple for dull books: many of them won't sell for months, years (some may even take root, or worse, take a walk with the help of a thief). So if a library is worth approximately £10,000, it is perfectly fair to offer, say, £3,500, perhaps £4,000 for a really good all-round collection. But it is not all right, as some do, very cynically, to offer £1,000. That's plain mean. And stupid. Of course, you might get away with it, but equally you could find your host reaching for the electric carving knife; and if you end up a human fountain (eat your heart out, Sam Peckinpah), you have only yourself to blame.

It's swings and roundabouts. Sometimes, as I say, with people who tell you what they want, and are delighted when they get it, you can do quite well. Just as often, however, I have known from the start that I am dealing with a very difficult person,

PRIVATE LIBRARIES

someone who *over*-estimates his library, thinks he's got a gold-mine (when it's strictly EPNS).

'Hello. You're the book people? Follow me. The books are in the dining-room. I should tell you straight away that I don't like comedians. I had some chap in here the other day who wanted to pay me a thousand for the lot. Pure satire. You see that book there, the hunting book by Selous, that one alone is worth £200. You're familiar with it, I presume? Good. Well, I hope you know your stuff, and I don't have to send you packing as well. And do take your time, study the editions carefully, sit down by all means, because if there's one thing I can't abide it's people in a hurry, *stand-up* comedians. Yes, if I can give you one piece of advice, try not to be funny—you'll find my sense of humour seriously limited.'

OK, so Mr EPNS (let's call him Everett Pilkington Nesbit Smythe) has a few good books, but what he fails to take into consideration is the state they're in. I must reiterate something I mentioned earlier: there are only three important factors in the second-hand book trade: condition, condition and condition. Now, reader, will you please memorise these three words for me (it doesn't matter if you get the order wrong). For it is a constant frustration (not to say disappointment) to view perfectly reasonable libraries in a state of decline. Sometimes it is a question of water or tobacco staining, or the sun has made the colour run or warped the boards; just as often it is something far more systematically appalling. I refer here to the inscription of one's name in pen, or the sticking down of a bookplate on the pastedown or front endpaper. There is an even worse habit, especially among older readers, of buying new hardbacks and then throwing the dust-jackets away. This is barbaric: the human equivalent would be to flay someone while still alive. A false analogy, you will say, and yet we talk of a book having a certain shelf-life; well, so long as it does, it requires its protective outer skin. When reading a hardback, the thing to do is to lay the dust-jacket to one side as it tends to slip about and can get easily damaged; when you have finished, replace it, not only to keep the dust off, but to retain the value of the book.

I once viewed a library of fiction including several (potentially) expensive first editions. Not only did I curse quietly to myself when I came up against row after row of wrapperless books, imagining in my mind's eye the ritual binning over the years of their all-important covers; I was also presented with a surgeon's mask (I kid you not) and plastic gloves with which to handle the dust-laden items concerned. Very considerate I'm sure, but if he had treated his books properly in the first place, (a) they would have been less filthy, and (b) he would have been more so—filthy rich, I mean. Yes, even after dealing with me. I get exasperated at such moments, not only at the devaluation of the library for my purposes, but at the financial deprivation these people inflict on themselves. Don't get me wrong: dust-jackets don't greatly increase the value of just any book, only in some cases; but they're almost always a good idea, if only for improving the look of one. I won't go into the exceptions to the rule: the bookseller will know which he can throw away with impunity, so leave it to him!

The trouble is that even if people do know about the golden rule of good condition, they don't seem to know what fits the bill. You can hammer on at them about dust-jackets but they tend to look at you with a faint smile of distrust, a just-who-is-this-guy-trying-to-con sort of look. To them, it's about dust and nothing more, otherwise it wouldn't be called a dust-jacket, now would it? The fact that books look naked without one, are essentially incomplete, means nothing to them. The result: I've had to make what seems a comparatively low offer (though it's actually a fair one), and I'm promptly shown the door. What did I do? I suppose it's just my luck evening out. And it's remarkable how often generosity is rewarded in this way.

I went in once, the last of three dealers, to look at a small collection of modern books on theatrical history in Shakespeare's time. Good scholarly stuff, the usual Chambers' *Elizabethan Stage*, Henslowe's *Diary* and the like, the standard books on the subject. I looked them over very carefully, basing my calculations partly on the quality of the books, but at least as much on the stern expression of my host, a retired university professor. I made a fair offer—scrupulously so. With a pained expression he informed me that this was the best offer he'd had, at which point I relaxed ever-so-slightly; he then further informed me that it was not enough and would I be so good as to leave. Well, I was and I did—and if he'd called me up later with a change of heart I would not have returned. Unfortunately he didn't: my grand gesture of refusal was purely academic. So was he. Some people are never satisfied; they seem to expect you to pay more or less what the books are worth; the idea of profit is so vulgar to them it seems to have been ruled out altogether. No, my role in life is to give him back the money he has spent—that way I become a better human being.

I said, I went in last of three on this occasion; this is probably the best position to be in. If you go in first, second, even twelfth for that matter, you leave your bid with your host, and there is always the chance that whoever goes in last (i.e. when all the results are in) will be told the highest bid, and can then go one better. So if the top figure happens to be mine (say, £2,750), and the last person has offered a little less than that, the host can tell him the situation (just because he's there) and ask if he can match it. He can then hum and ha... well... I suppose I could make it a *little* more, how about £2,760?

Done: quite undeservingly, the books are his.

It is infuriating to be gazumped in this way—unless, of course, the last person is myself, and it's I who get the opportunity... suddenly, somehow, that doesn't seem quite so unfair. Where money's concerned, it seems, we're all capable of the worst kind of hypocrisy. Objectively speaking, shall we say then, the seller should bear in mind the hard work and experience that have gone into each offer, and give the library to the highest bidder. In a perfect world, that is. Naturally I appreciate that just as I am trying to get the best deal for the firm, the seller is doing the same at his end. Everyone has his own morality and sense of justice. My own rule is to try and deal with people as fairly as is consistent with business; I suppose I expect the same in return.

The better the books, of course, the more I offer. If it's a thoroughly mixed assortment, I've evolved my own approach—paying one price for the lot (including all the dead weight), and an appreciably higher one if I can select what I want, sometimes only half the library. (I refer you back to my nightmare catalogue of Chapter 4; the way I look at it, some books are actually negative equity.) Picking what you want is always easier; just as often, however, the deal is that you take everything and save *them* the task of dispatching the rubbish. It is a crying shame that all books are not worth something; but this is how it is, and even the best libraries have dead weight in them. No one can know, at the time of purchase, what books will be collectable fifty years from then.

Visiting private libraries may well be an adventure, but potentially at least it's a dangerous one. Fortunately I don't have any stories of the Suzy Lamplugh variety; but it's quite true, when you get that call, you don't really know who you're dealing with. And vice versa. An old lady answering the door must be wondering whether she can trust me, a complete stranger. Of course, I present a card, I'm carrying auction bags, and I have (so I'm told) an honest face—if anything, I'm a little *too* plausible. But seriously, if there's no particular reason why someone of the Dennis Nilsen school of hospitality should call me up, it's not impossible. Nothing has happened yet, nor—believe me—do I wish to fill a disaffected reader's head with antisocial ideas, revenge perhaps for being bored out of his mind over the last ten chapters. (It gets better: I know I said that earlier, but it does.)

And yet, now that I think about it, I did have an experience that verged on the Dostoyevskian.

I was once called to an obscure corner of South London. Only was it? On leaving the station I must have walked for over a mile, street after street after street, it was more like Hampshire before I arrived. Eventually I reached this house. I'd like to say it was straight out of the Bates Motel, or at least that it was dingy and decrepit, but on the outside it was perfectly ordinary.

Chap opened the door, military bearing, a shade withdrawn, no sign of any wife or child (either dead or alive). Family, I always think, is slightly reassuring—OK, there were the Wests, but *usually* ... So far so not very good then. A dim and dreary hallway, a rather cold, uninviting ambience, I'm beginning to feel distinctly less at ease. Then out of the blue a line straight from a Hammer horror movie:

'The books, I'm afraid, are in the cellar.'

What?

'Oh... right. After you then.'
'No no, Mr Davis. After *you*.'

And now, just as a drowning man sees his whole life flashing past him, romantic flings and all, I, O.J.M. Davis, bookseller, on the verge of decapitation, not to mention dismemberment and cannibalism (preferably in that order), see all the books I have flirted with flash past. One in particular arrests my attention: I re-enter the nightmare world of *The Idiot*, page after page unravels before me, until I arrive at the moment in which the simple hero Prince Myshkin, walking up a darkened staircase, is confronted by the eyes of the homicidal Rogozhin, gleaming at him from the shadow of a doorway. And here was I going *down* the stairs, without even the benefit of visual anticipation, my lugubrious host in cold pursuit. The more I felt his presence, the more he was like something out of the Addams Family.

I am dramatising after the event, you will say; my conjuring up of images from literature, cinema, and now even a cartoon strip reveals my desperation. And it's quite true that while I thought every second might be my last, I also thought I was being ridiculous, he was probably just one of those painfully repressed, ex-public school, ex-army types—yeah, the ones who become man-eating psychopaths in later life! Descending the steps, I thought, too, how much I had enjoyed reading Dostoyevsky, all the more because it was the characters who were suffering and not myself sitting in the armchair at home; I thought how much I'd like to be sitting there now, yes, *reading* Dostoyevsky, not living out one of his most suspenseful scenes. And then I reached the cellar and... relief.

Why? Well, there were no skeletons there for a start, no stench of decomposition—and there were stacks of books, too, arranged on the floor. Now he might have gone to the trouble of providing authentic props before closing in for the kill, but you can turn anything to your advantage. After all, I considered, if there were no books here, I could be sure I was in for the chop, but as there were ... The cellar was not well lit, there were no chairs, I had to squat right down to examine them, and I had to do this while Lurch stood at attention behind me— rigor was clearly setting in. I felt about as relaxed as anyone would in a common-or-garden torture chamber. The books weren't up to much, I made my offer, packed them up in haste, scurried up the stairs ahead of him, and then I was out of there, counting all my limbs (four, fantastic), amazed to find myself, well, if not in mint, at least near-fine condition.

In the taxi I'm thinking, quite an ordinary bloke really, not much of a sense of humour perhaps, still, what a fuss, I mean, most people are not serial killers, I've never even met *one*. Too much reading, that's what does it (books—who needs them?), bloody Dostoyevsky, this isn't the land of the Tartars, this is drab, quotidian London, a harmless conglomeration of high streets and shopping malls, supermarkets and fast-food outlets. (And yet, there's no getting away from Dennis Nilsen, for did he not serve up some of the fastest food in history?)

Yes, and it's also, as anyone who does regular house calls will tell you, the land of old widows who have large libraries to sell you, only, when you arrive, they're remarkably short on books, and long on memories, which they wish to share with you ('such a nice young man'), now that they're alone, over multiple cups of tea and biscuits.

Six months later—no, you're not still there—but you've

barely recovered from the ordeal when your widow rings up again. She's discovered to her great surprise (how short-sighted she's getting) that there's another load of hubby's cricket books tucked away in a wardrobe, so you're back at the wicket, stoutly defending against further deliveries of riveting suburbia, and renewed onslaughts of tea and biscuits. The nice young man retires hurt, and fervently trusts that in six months' time no startling discoveries are made in the sock drawer—don't worry, he checked it out when her back was turned. Perhaps by then the nice old lady will in any case have choked on the ginger snaps and taken up cosy residence in the same celestial pavilion as her dearly departed (oh, and equally nice) husband.

It's also the land of fifty-going-on-seventy-five casualties of the 1960s generation, husky, frazzled, user-friendly women who invite you upstairs to see their books (and—you hope—nothing else) with a wince-inducing smile, and a flutter in the eyes as false as their lashes used to be.

And of brusque wine columnists who tell you exactly what they expect for their books, and when you offer (more realistically) less than half the amount, spit you out of the house with the same dyspeptic contempt they show for a lousy vintage.

Oh, and did I mention the old man who told me he had a thousand books to sell, and then when I turned up at his door, shamelessly informed me he'd had a change of heart, and was leaving his books to charity? Obviously he had never heard of the telephone (even though he was probably alive when it was invented), or just plain good manners, but as I've always been told to respect my elders and betters, I can only conclude, being younger and worse, that it was my fault.

Nor have I exhausted all the possibilities. No, these stories I've been telling you are mere drops in the ocean, hors-d'oeuvres with which to whet the appetite, compared to the main course which follows...

12

A to Z

The assistant manager was still pacing about. 'You know, it's three days since that call, and my back's aching even now.'

Claire was nothing if not plain-speaking. 'Why don't you sit down, then?'

'*Someone* has to check over the stock.'

They all exchanged brief glances. If only the manager wasn't away, their eyes seemed to say in unison, but was a tyrant any better than a martyr?

'Someone has to go out buying, someone has to view the auctions, and someone has to look after the shop.'

'Could it be in that case,' and Claire alone could get away with this, 'that someone is going to be seriously pissed off?'

'If only Simon wasn't away.'

'Yes, we were thinking—' but Claire kicked Paul before he could finish.

'Of all the weeks to be ill, he had to choose—'

'Choose?' Malcolm challenged. 'Not everything goes according to plan.'

'Hmm. Just think: right now he's probably lying on his back...'

Malcolm bit his lip. 'Peter, why don't you sit down?'

Peter sat down. He really did look tired. His physical relief was theirs.

'If you'd only delegate more,' suggested Claire. Of course, she knew that he liked being important, but even she baulked at saying this.

He didn't hear her. 'You know, it's amazing. Despite that call, we're still short of books. I've been looking around. There are gaps everywhere.'

'Do you want to do another, then?' teased Claire.

'Don't tempt fate.'

'Oh, I doubt if anything I say—'

The phone rang. Peter nearly jumped. He looked at everybody in turn, and they looked at him. It rang again. It might have sent twinges through his shoulder blades, he was rubbing at them so hard. And again. Peter just stared at it.

'Me and my big mouth,' said Claire. Ring-ring. 'It could just be a simple inquiry, though. Normally you're so keen to answer.'

'I know. But there are days when—' (ring-ring) '—and this is one of them.'

Clearing his throat, taking a deep breath, he moved over to the phone on a side desk, and as he picked it up, tuned his voice into a professional mode.

'Hello. Aardvark Books ... That's quite right, we do.' His face fell; he pursed his lips at Claire; and then he rubbed his back again. 'You're speaking to the buyer, madam. Uh huh, and what do you...? You got there before me.' He started taking notes. 'Right... yes... uh huh... I see. It does sound like the sort of thing...'

'He's depressed,' said Claire. 'It must be good.'

'Ah, that was going to be my next ... Several hundred, you say. We certainly can. The only question is when. I mean, this week ... What! Today! But we can't possibly... I mean, that's cutting it a bit fine, isn't it? It doesn't give us much... are you sure it has to be...'

There was a long pause during which Peter examined his sore left hand.

'Stigmata,' Claire whispered mischievously to Malcolm.

'I see.' His tone was sepulchral. 'The trouble is, one of us is off sick,' he floundered on. 'It's not a very convenient ... No no, I didn't say we *couldn't*... did I say...?'

'You didn't,' Claire encouraged him.

'Not a bit of it,' confirmed Paul.

Peter waved them away. 'I just need to think this through. I suppose I could always... yes, I'll have to call... sorry, just thinking aloud here. I'm sure something can be arranged.'

'After what he's been saying,' whispered Malcolm, 'how can he even contemplate it?'

'You have to admit he's got stamina.'

'Look, does it really have to be today?' Peter went on.

'Uh uh, he's faltering,' Malcolm sniggered.

'No no, I'm sorry, of course it does, as you say, what with moving, and someone else not turning up... to clear them... I do understand, I'll just have to... never mind what I'll have to do.' He laughed fakely. 'You don't want to hear about that, after all.' He laughed again.

'My God!' Malcolm seethed.

'Yes. Let's say one o'clock. There we are: now I'll *have* to come. Just kidding. Don't worry, we're very reliable, in fifteen years I've never missed an appointment.'

'Oh spare us,' said Claire. 'The worst thing is, it's true.'

'Do you have any boxes? You do? Fine. Sounds like we'll need a lot of them. The same ones... when you moved in... how clever of you. Such foresight.'

'*Forsyte Saga*, more like. This is interminable.'

'Does she sound pretty or something?' said Paul.

'I expect so. Why else would he bend over backwards to be so charming?'

'Is that what you call it?' queried Malcolm.

'OK. I've got the address. And may I ask where you heard about us? Helps with the advertising ... Right you are. Thank you. See you soon.'

Peter hung up. He came away from the desk rubbing his hands.

'Well...' he said by way of introduction.

'You seem disarmingly cheerful all of a sudden.'

'Claire, I think we're onto a winner.'

'But surely—' Malcolm began.

'Don't tell me,' Peter put up his hand, 'I made a fuss, but you know how it is when the work catches up with you. And I don't say this won't be painful too. But what can you do? She's got history, biography, all hardback, bought new, and in good condition. She was very precise; even gave me a few titles.' He paused. 'Oh, and there's... something else.'

They knew it must involve some cleverness of his, for he smiled at them all one by one, like a prompter cueing an ensemble.

'Yes?' It was amazing how much reluctance Claire put into this word.

'Why did she choose us? Well?'

'Could it possibly be...' Malcolm began—Peter nodded him on—'...Aardvark Books?'

'Eureka! That snuffling old aardvark has come up trumps again: first in the directory, works every time.'

'And whose idea was that?' Claire put in with ritual irony.

'My dear, if half of you is made of salt, the other half... is pure sugar.'

'Icky-icky. You are in a good mood.'

'The aardvark, I confess it, was my idea,' and he twiddled his tie in self-parody. 'Even though I haven't a clue, to this day, what an aardvark is.'

'Is it not... just occasionally...?'

'A bothersome little thing? How discreet you are, Malcolm. No, I'm not denying we get the odd freak call. Do you remember that woman who had a library of natural history books; was that in our line, she asked, or was it *only* books on aardvarks?'

Claire shook her head with compassion.

'Malcolm, these people will always exist. If we took too much account of them, we'd never get anywhere.' He clapped his hands. 'Now we have to get shipshape. I've agreed to a one o'clock appointment. I'll need you with me this time; there are too many books for one person. You're in charge here, Claire; Paul, keep your wits about you; and I'd better call Lucy, I did warn her she might have to do overtime, she can cover for your lunch-breaks.'

* * * * *

Peter's high spirits were dampened a little when he got out of the cab.

'Hmm. It's one of those modern apartment blocks set back from the road. How are we going to get a van in there?'

'We haven't got the books yet.'

'Be positive, Malcolm, that's what I always say. If you believe in something enough, it'll be yours.'

If only... for at such moments Malcolm wanted to believe in giant birds of prey that swooped down and carried off booksellers with reach-me-down philosophies. Peter was too busy surveying the scene on the ground, however, to notice Malcolm looking skyward.

'The caretaker's over there by the barrier, there's a ramp to let cars in, the van could come up and around to the forecourt, good, yes, I'm sure he could park here for a while. Right, this is the block we want. Number 28.' He pressed a buzzer, waited a moment, then spoke into the intercom. 'Hello. Aardvark Books. Third floor? Thank you.'

Going up in the lift, 'Let's hope we don't have to take it all,' said Malcolm.

'Well, I don't like it any more than you do,' replied his superior—the tone made Malcolm think he was about to be caned—'but if we have to oblige the lady we will. We're an established firm, Malcolm, we state in our ad that we can take everything, we have our reputation to think of.'

AARDVARK BOOKS—BOOKSELLERS TO THE QUEEN, Malcolm conjured mischievously, as they arrived, with a jolt, at the third floor.

'This lift's a bit iffy.'

'Now now,' said Peter.

Oh yes, he was being negative again. He couldn't help it. It was a day-to-day grind of hard, cheerless work, he was rarely consulted when it came to important decisions, and he was still on the lowest pay of anyone in the shop, with the exception of Paul and Lucy, who were only part-time anyway. As Peter strode out purposefully in front, Malcolm shuffled at a slower pace behind, hanging his head. They followed the arrow for number 28 down the corridor, then they turned a corner, and walked along, and along, right down to the end of the second corridor.

'Why is it always...?' Peter checked himself.
'Now now,' Malcolm smiled.
Pressing the bell, Peter pursed his lips.
When the door was opened, 'Jennifer Caldwell?' he breezed. 'Aardvark Books. I'm Peter Dawes, and this is my colleague, Malcolm Illingworth.'
They all shook hands. The woman was a little older than Peter had anticipated—voices could be so deceptive—early forties like himself.
'Excellent. You're very punctual.' Then under her breath: 'Unlike some people I could mention.' Setting off with remarkable speed, 'The books are through here,' she announced, and with no more ado was tearing off down the hallway, again right to the end, and into a large sitting-room. They stood between two walls lined with books. 'As you see, they're arranged chronologically. The first block there is medieval history, then Elizabethan, Stuart, Hanoverian and so on. The military is on the opposite wall, arms and armour in the first two bays there, English Civil War, Napoleonic, First and Second World Wars, and... well... other.'
'Very methodical.'
'Yes. Very.'
'Mrs Caldwell—'
'Jennifer,' she brusquely corrected.
'Excuse me. Naturally I assumed—' Malcolm winced at Peter's outmoded gallantry. 'I meant to say... is this everything?'
'Oh... how foolish of me.'
'Something about biographies?'
'Quite. They're in the dining-room. Follow me please.'
And they did. She had the crisp authority of a tour guide. She would suffer no nonsense from visitors, Malcolm instinctively felt. Would she hit it off with Peter in that case, a man who, as far as he was concerned, trafficked quite extensively in that commodity?
As they traipsed back down the hallway, Peter peered into one of the rooms leading off it.
'That's my son's, I'm afraid. Forgive the bomb-site. Teenagers, you know.'

'I sympathise,' he smiled. 'I have two of my own. My eldest—'

'The books are in here,' she cut him off. 'As you see, biography, two shelves of hardback fiction, all strictly alphabetical.'

'Very organised.' Peter nodded with satisfaction. And there was really nothing more to say. Except that, being Peter: 'You certainly know how to—'

'Thank you. I can leave you to it? I'm sure you'll want to get on.'

'Oh... absolutely.'

'In fact, I'm keen to get on myself. I don't want to sound rude, but I require the speediest possible inventory.' Malcolm blinked: for a moment he thought she'd said 'infantry'. It wouldn't have been out of place; as it was, they were practically under marching orders. 'Obviously I want a square deal,' she continued, 'but please make an offer, well, as soon as you can.'

'Certainly. We'll do our best.' He added irrelevantly: 'Won't we, Malcolm?'

Peter was trying to be inclusive—but the end result was patronising. He merely nodded in answer.

'You don't say much,' she observed.

Malcolm, however, did not respond. He sensed a rebuke. He was prepared to admit that if Peter talked too much, then he ... But why should she want him to speak if she was in such a hurry? For reassurance? It was true that his lugubriousness could have a disconcerting effect.

'Well, if you need anything...' And then she was gone. Only to pop her head back almost immediately. 'Sorry. Would you like some tea? Or coffee perhaps?'

'Not for me, thanks,' said Peter.

The tone was his most martyred, most sternly professional. Malcolm would have none of it. 'Tea with two sugars,' he spoke up for himself. When something *needed* to be said...

They soon got down to the job of assessing the books. Peter made a few notes as he went along, checked out some of the more expensive items, counted the books on a number of shelves.

'Just as she described. I knew it would be straightforward.'

'She seems awfully nervous.'
'Really? I find her very efficient.'
'It's some sort of smokescreen. Didn't you notice her palm was wet?'
'Well, she's good reason to be nervous: she's alone with two strange men.'
'It's not that.'
Peter was taken aback by his unusual emphasis. 'What then?'
'I don't know. I can't put my finger on it.'
'But you'd like to.'
Malcolm frowned: even when Peter was being fruity he was irritating. And sex was the last thing on his mind: if anything, her guillotine voice had a castrating effect. As for the 'two strange men' theory, he must at least amend it to one, for he exempted himself.
'How's it going?' Jennifer appeared with the tea.
'Very well,' Peter looked up. 'You've made it easy for us. Nothing out of place.'
'That figures.'
'Sorry?' She shook her head. 'And it's a truly comprehensive library. I think you have excellent taste.'
'Me? You must have gathered... from the strong military presence, that is... they're—'
'Your husband's?' Peter interrupted.
'Precisely.'
The smile showed how pleased he was to be right. 'As I say, a man of excellent taste.' He positively beamed. Malcolm did not miss the ambiguity; however, he rather hoped that she did.
'Yes. Yes, I suppose he... was.'
'Oh. That is... oh, I *am* sorry.'
'Not at all.'
'You do mean...?'
'Mean? Oh yes. It's just...' she actually shrugged her shoulders '... one of those things.'
'I don't know what to say.' He didn't know where to look either. Somehow death had never occurred to him. He was genuinely shocked.
'I'll let you get on.'

'No. I mean... yes, we won't be long now.'

They moved back to the first room; they worked on in silence for a while.

'How many books, would you say?' said Malcolm. 'Didn't she estimate in the low hundreds?'

'Yes. It's more. Between eleven and twelve.'

'That's very exact.'

'Well, after fifteen years...'

Malcolm nodded: after such a time he supposed that even he might end up acquiring a little pride in his knowledge—if not, he hoped, to the point of complacency.

'How was I to know?'

To give him his due, he also admitted his faults.

'She didn't mention it before?' Malcolm helped him.

'I suppose it wasn't relevant. Poor woman. She's very attractive, don't you think? An awful blow at her age. And with a child too. Still, it explains her... edge.' Malcolm frowned. 'You don't seem convinced.'

'No no. I expect you're right.' As he idly turned over a leaf, 'Oh look. Isn't that Montgomery's signature?'

'Malcolm, I do believe ... Well found. Well found indeed.'

He was beginning to think Peter wasn't so bad after all; he was happy enough to praise him when he did something right.

'I've been meaning to have a word with Simon, you know, about your salary.'

Could it be that the insufferable Peter was actually his bestest, bestest friend? What a disturbing thought! And one that was fortunately interrupted by the ringing of the phone in her bedroom next door.

'You again?' came muffled. 'But I've already told you ... There's nothing *to* discuss. No means no, can't you get that into your thick skull?... Oh I haven't got the patience, this is not the time, OK? There never will be a ... There's no point in ... Oh, go to blazes!' And with that she slammed the phone down.

Peter looked at Malcolm. 'What on earth...?'

'Sounds like a lovers' tiff.'

'She is unlucky.'

Steps approached once more. 'Making progress?' asked

Jennifer. But if her tone was bright, her face was even more so, inflamed as it was with strawberry blotches.

'Are you OK?' asked Peter. 'I know it's none of my business—'

'Oh that. You must forgive me. I just would have thought,' she looked him directly in the eye, 'that after several refusals these people would stop their persecution.' She turned to Malcolm now. 'Double bloody glazing.'

'The bastards,' said Peter. 'I mean... pardon my—'

'No,' she reverted to him. 'That's just what they are. They will not stop ringing. They've even got a stupid jingle: 'Blah-blah and Blah: Words for Windows'. But there's no noise here. And it's not as if there are any draughts. The way they keep on, you'd think I'd die of pneumonia.'

'*Double* pneumonia.'

'Malcolm!'

'No, that's very good.' She mulled over it. 'Hilarious, in fact.' She didn't laugh. 'But let's drop it. Have you nearly done now? You see, I've got some furniture people coming at four.'

'I quite understand. Yes, I think so. Have you finished, Malcolm? Good. A solid library then, you said "several hundred" books I think, is that right, yes, well, I estimate maybe 650.' He turned to his colleague. 'What do you say?'

Malcolm's hand levitated in the air.

'700 then—it's always more than you think anyway. Did you, er, have a price in mind?'

'No. Not at all. I was rather hoping that you...'

'Of course. Very proper. Well, it's a good working library, a few slow ones too inevitably, some that hang around like unwanted guests—I do hope we haven't "hung around" too long,' he laughed (Malcolm seethed), 'you did say you were in a hurry? Three thousand it is then.'

In fact, the price was delivered at bullet speed; too fast even for Jennifer, who looked for a moment as if she'd been shot. Malcolm was worried; Peter, on the other hand, swore inwardly, for he knew at once he could have got away with less.

'Is that, er, satisfactory?' he filled up the pause.

'But are you sure that's not too much?'

Peter was quite sure. And he had anticipated such a reaction.

Surviving spouses often felt uncomfortable, guilty even, taking money for their dead husband's possessions.

'Right then,' she recovered. 'Let me show you where the boxes are.'

'You *are* efficient. I sometimes wish my wife—'

'I've also got some brown tape and a Stanley knife.'

'Excellent. Malcolm, why don't you get started while I make out the cheque? Now, Jennifer, who shall I make it payable to?'

She seemed to hesitate; she was in a bit of a daze again.

'The cheque,' he repeated. 'You weren't expecting cash?'

'Of course not,' she laughed. 'To me of course.'

'Jen-ni-fer Cald-well,' he spoke it out loud as he wrote it. 'Three... thousand... pounds. That's the bit I don't like. Huh huh. Right. There we are.'

When he turned round to give it to her she was practically standing over him; his hand brushed ever-so-slightly against her breast.

'Don't lose it now,' he joked, trying to hide his embarrassment.

'No danger of that.'

The words were almost mercenary. How she confused him! One moment she seemed reluctant, the next...

There was a momentary tension in the room.

Dispelling the *frisson*, 'I expect you'll want to get on,' she encouraged him.

'Absolutely. Do you mind if I make a couple of calls? You see, I'm going to need a van for this lot.' She looked at him in alarm. 'Don't worry, it won't be long. Then I need to call the shop to tell them when to expect it.'

'Fine. And I'll have a word with the man on the gate. He needs some warning.'

Things continued to go smoothly. After booking a van, and being joshed by Claire about last-minute hitches (didn't the woman want to write hubby's name in all the books before letting them go?), Peter joined Malcolm, and set to work packing up. The latter couldn't help being impressed by the speed of his colleague. Peter was so rhythmic, so well coordinated, straightening out each box, biting off a strip of tape to seal the bottom, cramming books into every inch of space, then another bite, the top was sealed, and he was taking it out in the hallway ready for removal. Box after box after box were handled with the same expertise, Peter managing about three to Malcolm's two, even whistling old Beatles tunes while he worked. Malcolm was capable enough himself, but he had less energy in reserve, which tallied well with his inverted view of capitalism: the less you earned the less work you should do. Besides, Peter built up a momentum, seemed actually to enjoy all this; profit, or the prospect of it, was grist to his mill. So Malcolm plodded methodically on, while Peter pumped up the adrenalin.

'Still bothered?' he asked, launching into another bite. 'I grant you she's a little odd,' he smoothed the tape over the crease, 'but bereavement takes people in very strange ways.'

As if to prove the point, the phone had been ringing for some time, but apparently she declined to answer it.

When they had packed up the books in the dining-room, they moved on to the living-room. It was a humid day, and rather airless in the flat; they were both getting uncomfortably warm.

'I've simply got to have a rest,' said Malcolm, sitting on a box.

'Man must work by the sweat of his brow,' said Peter sententiously.

'My brow I can cope with. It's my shirt that's sodden.'

Peter tapped Malcolm on the arm. 'Heh, how about this? "Soddenly",' he began to croon into an imaginary microphone, "I'm not half the man I used to be".'

He laughed. Malcolm seethed.

Dozens of boxes were lining the hallway by now, stacked three high, but there were as many more to fill. As their tempo began to slow, Jennifer came in to check up on them more and more. She seemed anxious to get it all sorted out as quickly as possible, even though the furniture dealers weren't due for a good two hours.

The phone rang again; once more she ignored it.

'Double glazing?' suggested Peter.

'Who else? It's become one big joke to them. They're no better than obscene phone callers.' And her blotches returned.

As they wilted more and more under the strain, she started packing up a box herself, lifting the books in very gingerly, one or two at a time, arranging them to her satisfaction, then sealing the box thoroughly as if it contained fragile antiques. Peter and Malcolm exchanged amused glances at the 'feminine' touch. Actually it was something in the nature of a performance: she would have liked to be more ruthless, only the books were theirs now, and she mustn't damage them. When she attempted to lift it, however, she staggered slightly; Peter moved swiftly to help.

'Really I can manage,' she said, in a tone that verged on irritation.

'No no, I insist,' he replied, even bowing before taking it from her.

Malcolm thought his colleague missed the hint of the incendiary altogether.

When Peter came back from the hall, she had already started on another.

'You must let me contribute; I just want to speed up the process, that's all.' Her voice began to quaver a little. 'You see, I want these books out of here, they... upset me so.' And such was the pressure of this sudden emotion that she almost flung the last few in.

'Anything that reminds you—'

'Exactly. So... please,' her hand, grasping the tape and Stanley knife, was practically trembling now, 'just let me get on with my bit. All right?'

She sealed the box, gathered it up, staggered again, and it took an abrupt shake of the head from Malcolm to prevent Peter making the same mistake twice.

'She's quite deranged,' he whispered.

'Have a heart. The poor woman's taken an awful blow.'

At that point they could hear the approach of a loud, throbbing engine, then the slam of a door, and when they heard the buzzer they knew the van had arrived. In good time: they only had a few boxes to go.

'Is he here? Excellent. Why don't you start loading up while I finish off?'

'Would you?' said Peter. 'But that's awfully kind.'

Malcolm watched her produce an impossible smile—it was far too broad to be genuine, a sort of actressy, face-lifted smile, entirely manufactured. He realised that her desperation was increasing; for whatever reason, the books must be out of there forthwith. He could see she just didn't have time for Peter's courtesy, and as he stood there transfixed by what he thought was her game spirit, Malcolm practically whirled him away into the hall, towards the mountain range of boxes that had to be shifted.

To the sound of Jennifer tearing off some tape, they heaved up a box each, clutched it securely, and started their tedious journey—through the glare of the strip lighting down the deadening length of the corridor, then, swerving round the corner into the second corridor, and on, and on, until they reached the lift. Then back down the corridor, swerving round the corner into the second corridor, and on, and on, down to the last door on the left, tramp, tramp up the hallway towards the waiting pile of boxes, a heave and a clutch, and tramp, tramp down the hallway, back into the glare of the strip lighting, down the deadening length of the corridor, a swerve and into the second corridor, along to the lift and... repeating this ritual over and over again, except now there were three of them, the van driver had joined in.

When they had collected some fifteen boxes, they jammed the lift doors open with one of them, and started piling them up inside, filling all the available space, though leaving enough room for the three of them. Then they descended in the lift, landed with a jolt on the ground floor, jammed the doors open once again, while they emptied all the boxes out into the lobby. Next they jammed the entrance door into the lobby open, while taking the boxes out down a short flight of stairs into the forecourt, and across to the van whose rear door was open. The driver got up into it, taking each box in turn as Malcolm and Peter handed it up to him, and carrying them deep inside to allow room for the rest that were to follow. The first batch thus deposited, they shambled back up the steps, through the lobby to the lift, and rode up again to the third floor, arriving once more with a jolt. Then they walked down the corridor, turned into the second corridor, entered through the front door, up the hallway, and launched into the second batch.

The phone rang.

It was only as they were going out that she answered it.

'You again. Yes yes, I'm perfectly aware ... That's right...deliberately. What? But that's quite impossible. I forbid you, do you hear?'

'Lovers' tiff?' smiled Bill, the van driver.

'That's what Malcolm said. No, apparently she has a problem with some double glazing people.'

'Look, just fuck off!' Jennifer concluded.

'Sounds to me like *they've* got a problem.'

They went down the corridor, turned into the second corridor, and came to the lift. They repeated this process several times, and on each return to the flat found Jennifer in even more of a state: egging them on, asking them how much longer, when the dwindling number of boxes was perfectly visible.

'She doing a runner or something?' Bill persisted, pressing the button for the lift, then once again jamming the doors open with a box.

Malcolm considered this literally. 'Isn't that done in darkness?'

Ever the gentleman, 'She's very highly strung,' Peter defended.

Having deposited this second batch safely into the van, they rode up in the lift again, breathless, dizzy, their calf muscles burning. When they tumbled out onto the third floor they met with a surprise: several boxes were already stacked beside it. Jennifer must have carried them there herself.

'Ah! That makes life easier,' said Bill.

Malcolm nodded in agreement. 'And yet I can't say I like it.'

Peter was furious. 'No. These boxes are far too heavy for a woman.'

'I wasn't referring to that.'

Negotiating the two corridors once more, backwards and forwards, Malcolm was thinking how the exact shade of grey-green carpet would be engraved on his mind forever, together with the numbers on the doors, 25, 26, 27 (or, conversely, 27,

26, 25), the Yellow Pages directory still sitting on a mat from a recent delivery, and the slight stain on the right-hand wall between 23 and 24 (the left-hand wall between 24 and 23). As far as he was concerned, these were not corridors where people lived—nobody had appeared all this time—but where a sentence of hard labour was being carried out. He hoped Peter was serious about his salary; if only for today's ordeal, he deserved it. All the more so as, when they had jammed the lift doors open for the third and last time, put in their load, brought the door-stop box inside and pressed the ground floor button... nothing happened. The lift did not respond. Press and punch and kick as they might, the damn thing was really jammed this time. Cursing their luck, the three tired men traipsed disconsolately back to the flat.

They found Jennifer walking up and down as if she were standing on hot coals, constantly glancing out the window. She nearly had a coronary when she heard the news.

'If this isn't the ... Oh I can't believe my ... Look, you'll just have to carry them down.'

'Can't the caretaker...?' Peter began.

'Out of the question! He's far too busy. Besides, it would take too long.'

'We won't be rushing it,' Malcolm warned her.

'And what's that supposed to mean?'

Peter frowned. 'Don't you worry. We'll be as quick as we can.'

Bill was even more optimistic. 'Like that,' he clicked his fingers.

After a quick glower at Malcolm, Jennifer rewarded the other two with another of her specials, this time a quivering, Shostakovich sort of smile. The glower was more palatable.

They returned at their different paces to the lift—Malcolm as usual at the rear—took all the boxes out of it, then one by one, box by box, they embarked upon a new route. Each floor, they soon discovered, consisted of two flights of stairs, with a landing in between, so down they went, one, two, three, straining under the weight, four, five, six flights of stairs, underarms odorous, drip-drip-dripping from their temples, then out through the lobby onto the porch, down that final flight, and stumbling over to the van with its back door open. Bill scrambled up as usual, took the boxes as far back as he could, then sprang down again, and all three walked up one, two, three, four, five, six flights of stairs to the remaining stack of boxes by the lift, wiped their brows, scooped up another box with a grunt, and proceeded to stagger down once more. Malcolm cursed the day he was born; even Peter's professionalism, which had remained intact until now, was coming apart at the seams. Though he had visibly disapproved of Malcolm's blunt remark to Jennifer, he had said nothing about it. As for Bill, he was a man made of iron, this was strictly everyday business. He was already calculating how many more jobs he would have to do that day, loading, unloading, loading, unloading. He had known for a long time that in this business he couldn't win: the faster he was, the more jobs could be fitted in, the more physical hardship; the slower he was, the more energy he conserved, and the less money.

Coming through the lobby with the final batch—just one wretched box remained in the flat—they met a man on his way in.

'What have you got there?'

'Books,' said Peter.

'Oh really. I didn't know anyone else round here could read.'

'Forgive us,' said Malcolm, wheezing past him, 'if we don't stop for a chat.'

'Of course.' Turning abruptly: 'Is the lift working today?'

Bill shook his head. 'Buggered, mate.'

Peter and Malcolm paused by the van, gasping for breath. Bill shifted things around inside.

'Do you read a lot yourself then?' the man called from the steps.

Peter found him just a shade supercilious. 'Now and again,' he discouraged.

'And you?' he turned to Malcolm. 'Do you like books?'

'Do I like pain in fact?'

The man gave a staccato laugh, stopped suddenly as if he had remembered something, peered at the box labels, shook his head, then went inside. Bill followed at his heels, going up nobly for the final box.

'I don't know why I'm laughing, I've got six flights of stairs to climb.'

'Ditto.'

The other two were left alone.

'Think of it this way,' Peter laid an avuncular hand on Malcolm's shoulder, 'the lift could have failed earlier.'

'But there's the other end,' he practically wailed in despair.

Peter sighed. 'Let's cross our bridges...' He was too disheartened to finish.

After another minute, 'Last time,' said Peter, as they gathered themselves up—they had to say goodbye and collect their jackets.

They went back into the building, up one, two, three, four, five, six flights of stairs—but why didn't they meet Bill coming down?—past the lift, down the first corridor, then, turning into the second corridor, heard a dreadful cacophony of voices coming from somewhere, till, approaching the door of number 28, they found the voices even louder, and Bill on the threshold shaking his head, and further on up the hallway a man leaning against the wall for support, and slumped on the floor against the opposite wall, Jennifer, pounding her knees in frustration. The man, the very same one who had quizzed them downstairs, was speaking, apparently to the carpet.

'It's not why. It's because.' And he shook his head. 'It's because you can do such things.'

The voice was high-pitched and yet male, apparently in control, but coiled up with a mixture of anger and indignation. As an unknown, unfamiliar quantity, Peter and Malcolm were completely hypnotised by it. The whole drama, in fact. They had stumbled unexpectedly onto a scene of carnage, and were powerless to deal with it. All they could do was watch in fascination, their hot sweat gradually turning cold. Only Bill was not quite so impressed; he pulled humorous expressions at the other two.

'You can do... such things.' (The "do" was falsetto; the "things" concluded with a teeth-clenching hiss.) 'Thank God I had to talk... this makes it all the more urgent.'

But she was equally angry. 'What do you expect?' If tearful.

'Fair play?' Snot dangled from her nose. 'After you and that... tartlet...'

'Leave her out of this!' But this was mere peremptory barking. 'Besides, she's almost your age.'

Her head jerked up. 'Then she ought to know better.'

'I said...' (and he shifted once more to his squeaky serpent's voice) '...please... leave her... out of this. I said it... and I meant it.'

'Tartlet!' She had all the appearance of a witch; she cackled even, then choked on her maniacal laughter, spluttering out tears instead.

The man shook his head.

'What on earth...?' Peter couldn't help expostulating.

'And may I say,' he suddenly turned to the three men—it was as if he had only just noticed them—'that your presence here is somewhat... supernumerary.'

He didn't reckon on Peter's pride. 'I demand to know—'

'What that means?' the stranger condescended.

Peter shut his eyes. 'I'm perfectly aware—'

'Apparently not.'

Bill turned to Malcolm. 'What the fuck does it mean?'

Malcolm put his finger to his lips.

'What it means...' The man curled his fist to his chin like Rodin's *Thinker*; except that he pressed it—and it hardly needed a deeper cleft—with pugnacious force. 'It means, my dear chap, that you are the most unfortunate man ever to walk this earth.' Before Bill could interrupt—not that he intended to quibble with the verdict—the man added: 'Oh, excluding me, of course.' He appealed to Jennifer: 'Is not the man quite seriously unfortunate?'

Still slumped, Jennifer scowled across at the serpent leaning against the opposite wall, as if he were the devil himself.

'What my... husband,' and she gagged on the word, 'is trying to say...'

'Husband?' Peter echoed. If not the devil, he was at least a ghost.

'Is that another difficult word to grasp?' She seemed to have forgotten that he was supposed to be dead. 'Husband, partner... in crime, if nothing else. What Roger—'and now she swivelled back and forth between them '—how I always hated that name, did you know that, Roger?—is trying to say, is that you are intruding—which is how I feel about you, you home-wrecker, snake-in-the-grass—and that the books...'

Peter's eyes goggled out of his head.

'... MUST-COME-BACK!'

Malcolm surprised everyone by yelping like a wounded animal.

'I imagine,' Roger focused on him now, 'that must have been strenuous work. Packing up *my* library, without *my* permission, and then taking it down, with the lift broken and all that... only down, mind you, just think how much worse it'll be coming up, I got quite puffed just now...'

'Don't be cruel, Roger.'

He stared at her in disbelief. 'You make me laugh.' He laughed as if to prove it. Mirthlessly. 'Did I invite—?'

'If you think—' Peter began.

'Think!' Roger moved away from the wall, and now slithered towards Peter. 'I should say I do think. And if you had *thought* (just for a moment) about the sort of wo-, no, she's a disgrace to her sex... *person* then, you were dealing with—'

'It was you,' said Malcolm, between shivering gasps, 'who married her.'

'Uh uh: an earlier version. What you see is the finished product.'

'And it was you who finished me.'

'Oh this is too much!' cried Peter. 'I don't want to hear this.'

'I ought to remind you, my dear chap, that I have the law on my side.' And now the cobra eyeballed Peter within striking distance. 'If you think I wouldn't call the police,' he prodded him, 'then let me tell you...'

'Take your hands off me,' Peter snarled.

'... if you think I wouldn't...' he prodded again.

Peter was practically foaming at the mouth; and as cobras generally steer clear of rabid dogs, Roger withdrew.

'And if you think I would,' spat Jennifer cryptically. 'He wants a divorce,' she explained to Peter. 'He'd have to kill me first.'

Roger countered: 'Maybe our visitors will oblige me.'

She actually looked puzzled for a moment. 'Oh, the books...' It was as if they had never been the issue.

Peter and Malcolm exchanged glances; they didn't know what to do. Then it suddenly occurred to them that the driver was no longer there.

'Where d'yer want 'em?'

It was Bill coming up the hallway clasping two boxes.

'But what are you doing?' said Peter.

'They're his, mate, aren't they?' he replied, with a nod at Roger. 'She's... it's a bitch, but that's what it comes down to.' In the same flat tone: 'Where d'yer want 'em?'

Roger had nothing to say; his venom was spent. Bill just dropped them where he stood.

Malcolm looked to Peter for guidance. 'Is he right?'

Without answering, Peter strode past them all into the bedroom, then popped his head back. 'All right to use your phone again?' he asked with mock deference.

Jennifer's lips trembled; she too was unable to speak.

After a moment, 'Claire, look, it's Peter,' came the tired voice. 'Yes, I'm afraid there's been a change of plan ... Well, the van—what can I say?—won't be coming, after all... I'll tell you exactly what I mean. The books belong to one Roger Caldwell, presumed dead, but regretfully, very much alive ... It's a good deal more than a spanner, my dear. So you see, strictly speaking, we're up the proverbial creek ... Oh yes, the whole shebang, no, I tell a lie, one box is still here, I must learn not to exaggerate ... But can I ask you, Claire, as someone I've known for many years now, why these things happen to me? Any ideas? I'm serious now ... Oh yes. Do you know I'd clean forgotten? Thank you, Claire, for reminding me.'

Peter returned to them, holding something behind his back.

'I believe you found us through Yellow Pages?' he inquired of Jennifer. She merely looked up at him in miserable defeat. 'May I flick through your copy?' He waved it in the air. 'I took the liberty...'

With the two principals punch-drunk, exhausted, only Malcolm was curious.

'Now let me see...' He turned over the pages until he found what he wanted. 'Where is it now? Ah yes: "Booksellers". Excellent. Oh look: what have we here, right at the top of the list? Aardvark Books. Well, wouldn't you know it. Tempting, that.' He turned to Malcolm suddenly. 'I just asked Claire,' (Bill brought in another two boxes) 'sterling work, Bill, we'll join you in a minute. Where was I? Oh yes—why these things happen to me. And do you know what she said? It's because I'm so damned clever. That was the gist of it anyway. I mean, Malcolm, if you looked up booksellers you'd start with 'A', especially Aardvark, goodness, what an intriguing name for a bookshop.' He spun round to Jennifer. 'Isn't that right?' And to Roger. 'I mean, wouldn't you?' The latter stared into space. 'No. Perhaps not. So you won't mind if I...'

Peter ripped the page out of the directory.

'Ah! That's better.' He came close to Roger now. 'A police matter perhaps? Damage to private property?'

Jennifer interrupted his glee. 'You're forgetting this.' She handed him the cheque.

'Oh no. I was hoping *you'd* forget. Then *I* could call the police.'

And once more they were tramping down the deadening length of the corridor, along and along, but while Peter swerved as usual, Malcolm kept on walking, and bang! hit his head, several times, against the end wall.

Without looking at Peter: 'Do you really feel better?' he questioned.

'Don't be ridiculous. But if that... swine can have his moment of triumph, then so can I.'

Malcolm seethed. Peter laughed.

The young man was at his lowest ebb, mentally as well as physically, for he realised his salary increase would be swept by the wayside now. Passing the mat with the Yellow Pages directory on it, he too picked it up, turned to the relevant page, and ripped it out. A gesture merely, but it expressed his solidarity: his colleague approved.

As they descended the first of the six flights of stairs, the stairs leading to hell, 'I've got it!' cried Peter, snapping his fingers.
'Got what?'
And he was inspirational. 'Zebra Books!'

13

The Second-hand Afterlife

Now if you thought that what I described in the last chapter was hell itself, you would be wrong; every bookseller's worst nightmare perhaps, but not hell. As I see it, every trade has its own eschatological scheme of things, and the second-hand book trade is no exception. Imagine a typical second-hand bookshop, with a first floor, a ground floor and a basement. Well, no prizes for guessing where hell's located. But, on closer inspection, this basement is not so typical, after all. For one thing, there is no light, or only just enough seeping through the crevices in the shuttered-up windows to reveal a far greater absence. The basement is stacked from floor to ceiling with shelves; there are walls of wood in every direction. Some carpenter must have made a supreme sacrifice (maybe it was *the* carpenter, on his harrowing visit) when he set up all this timber for nothing. I mean, he could have bought himself early retirement instead of choosing that more drastic method. But he wasn't being kind. These shelves, you see, are empty; there isn't a book in sight. And if you thought after the last chapter that there are times when a bookseller is glad to see the back of books, you were right, but only for a day or two, not forever. Soon he is hungry for more, good ones preferably, but if not that, then bad ones, any, something to remind him of what he is.

If hell in the Christian sense means the absence of God, then hell in the biblio sense is the absence of books. Something of their smell remains, of course, to tantalise the nostrils of the dwellers here; but it's not the appetising smell of polished bindings or quality art paper, more the whiff that comes off mildewed boards, or the vomit odour of recent American publications. And these bad odours mingle with the flatulence that besets so many people (as I mentioned earlier) who set foot in basements, the combined and prolonged flatulence of the thousands of occupants who throng these stinking premises. And this stink is compounded by the stench of unwashed anoraks and raincoats so beloved of a certain kind of collector who spends all his money on books but hasn't a penny left for the dry-cleaner's. But no quantity of anoraks is going to be enough to fend off the freezing draughts that come in with the light through those crevices, draughts that would have been so much less effective if those shelves had been filled with books, books that do insulate as well as furnish a room. And as they stand there in a shivering huddle, reeling from the miasma of each other's bodies, constantly scanning the shelves for a glimpse of book (like Columbus looking for land), the very thought of it is like the thought of food, and so they salivate, which unrequited drooling leaves a bad taste in the mouth. As for their fifth sense, this is amply abused by all the horrors of the modern world, those technological advances so detested by the serious reader: the constant bleeping of mobile phones, the monotonous drone of car alarms, the relentless throb of personal stereos blaring out a mixture of brain-damaging Spice Girls and motherfucking rap crap. For even if there are no books, it might have been possible to remember favourite lines of poetry, but these scraps of culture are lost in a perpetual assault on their eardrums, it is impossible to think under such conditions. Nor is their sixth sense left unscathed, for rumours constantly circulate about the floor above, purgatory, where books are believed to exist.

But this is not the end of it. After all, who are the unfortunate inhabitants of this bookless hypogeum? No, this is not the hot, colourful, Mediterranean hell of Dante, peopled with princes, popes and scholars, not to mention the downright diabolical, who exert at the very least a certain fascination:

'Who's that geezer over there giving off the serious vibes?'
'Why, that's Satan.'

'The Enemy of Mankind? Cor! You get a better class of person down here.'
'Didn't I tell you? Actually he's an angel, a real sweetie.'
'Do you think he'll take me under his wing?'
'Defo. Once you know your way about, it's not such a bad old place.'
'You're telling me. And to think he was my role model at school. What's he eating by the way?'
'He's on a modest diet these days: Judas, Brutus and Cassius—no carbohydrate.'
'Wow! Even the grub's good here.'
'You should try the medallion of Doge.'

Dream *on*: no such chance: this hell is altogether drabber and drearier. What do you expect? This is hell, second-hand book style, and it's peopled strictly with the second-rate—not the rarer master criminals, but the common or garden low life that belong to a bargain basement. (And their diet, naturally, is worms.) Let's see now, who do we have? For a start, every bookseller who ever bullied or cheated an old lady out of some private library for next to nothing; every runner who offered to sell a book on behalf of some guileless client and then was never seen again; every assistant who embezzled books out of his own company; every bibliomaniac who built a mountain of literature between himself and his family. All these are here, these and many more, guilty not only of crimes against humanity but worse, of book crime, abuse of a sacred object. They stumble around in the semi-darkness, or crawl about on all fours, constantly bumping into each other in the overcrowded space, desperately searching for the least glimmer of a spine or fore-edge, but all they ever encounter is these empty shelves, which whips them up into a frenzy of desperation, that and the half-sight of each other, the sickening glimpse of reprehensible faces. There is no need for devils to prod them with pitchforks, this hell is not so much painful as demoralising, the relentlessness of its digital sounds and smells—yes, even the smells are digital—filling its occupants with despair. And of course, these unfortunates are here till hell freezes over—so I said it was cold, well it isn't *that* cold.

Worst of all perhaps, because of their essentially corrupt nature, and in order to compensate for their booklessness, they cannot refrain from periodically boasting of their conquests and misdeeds; moreover the terrible babel of collective braying fills the already cacophonous room with an even greater volume of noise, increasing their torment. But even their most cherished memories of some book swindle or other are not left unsullied—pleasure, even of the retrospective kind, is an illusion here. No, their memory systems have been tampered with, so that just as they are about to recall the greatest scoop of their lives, a new ending is tacked on, and their braying turns to a horrified shriek. Here's one of them now, shouting out at the top of his voice to a group of reluctant listeners (for none of his fellow sufferers wants to hear of another's success):

'So this sucker of sixteen comes into my shop and says he's inherited a thousand books from his uncle. It's perfect, I tell you: his father ran away when he was young, his mother's hit the bottle big time, and there's this squirt with his head in the clouds, and no one to guide him. Then I'm taken into this frowsty old bachelor's study, and lo and behold, what do I see? Hundreds of bindings, a lifetime's collection, just sitting there on the shelves. Casually I turn to moon-face, "How much do you want for these?", my blood surging in secret, and this gullible twerp, do you know what he says, "Give me a fair price and take them off my hands"? I mean, who does he think he's dealing with, do I look like a saint?' (Frantic shakes of the head.) '"How about a thousand pounds?" I risk, barely able to keep a straight face—that's about a pound a book, for Satan's sake—and what do you think, "Fine," he says, "I'm happy with that". What a complete tit! So I'm home and dry, all that's left for me to do is pack them all up and... and... wait a minute, what's that terrible noise upstairs, oh shit, if I don't have the most infernal luck, a pipe must have burst, there's water pouring through the ceiling all over the shelves of books, can you believe it, bindings that have survived centuries, a hair's breadth from within my grasp, and in a matter of seconds they're... they're...'

He breaks off, sobbing uncontrollably, while the facial expressions of his listeners change from nausea to immense delight. But their *schadenfreude* is short-lived. Then it's the turn of the next one to recite his own unsavoury tale of meanness, and the next, the same thing happens with all of them, they come to the crunch, only to find the punch-line removed, the huge profit they made out of some shady deal obliterated, with only a nagging what-might-have-been remaining. Until it comes full circle, and our enemy recounts his story once more, he's unrepentant, you see, he will boast of his deceit to all eternity, they all will, and because their memories have been short-circuited, every time they come to their 'triumphant' conclusion they are overtaken by the same surprise. And so the cycle continues, every story making them salivate all the more, for each relates to that commodity so conspicuous by its absence.

* * * * *

Life on the ground floor, in purgatory, is very different. If hell is essentially a state of booklessness, purgatory is shelved from floor to ceiling with books. If hell is uniform, a state of equal misery for all its inhabitants, purgatory is hierarchical, and the different stages of penance are reflected in the varying quality of these books. In fact, the lowest of the low here, those who only escaped the other régime by the skin of their teeth, by some last-minute repentance of their dishonest actions, are still without books. These unfortunates are to be seen squatting on the floor, stretching out towards the books on the first shelf above their heads, inches, of course, beyond their grasp. But at least they can see them; their eyes, if nothing else, are delighted, they are incomparably better off than the sufferers below. And the terrible cacophony of subterranean sounds has yielded here to an anodyne dribble of piped music, a blotting paper of easy listening. In this state they sweat out their regrets until it is deemed fit for them to ascend to the next level.

Spanning the entire height of this enormous room is a gigantic ladder, with rung after rung thronged by repentant sinners, each level reflecting a different stage in the long slow process towards purification. The lowest rung of the ladder is opposite the bottom shelf of books, and once our friend has heaved himself up off the floor and clung to this, he is at last able to reach out and pick off a volume. But the books on this level, the ones he has been eyeing for ages in frustration, are little more than brain-teasers. Yes, when his fingers reach out towards the first one and grasp it, there is a moment of sweet gratification; but when he reads the title on the spine (written by hand in a humorous scrawl) his suspicions are aroused. What's this? *The Dodo in the Twentieth Century*. Surely ... He turns to page one—his heart sinks—it is blank. Frantically he turns to the next page, and the next, only to discover that all the pages are the same. In some trepidation he picks out the next book along: oh no, not *Obesity and the Fashion Model*, anything but that. A uniform whiteness throughout. As for the third, what have we here? For the love of Christ, he might have guessed: *The Sex Life of Immanuel Kant*—textless, virgin pure. It's no use: all the books on this shelf are similarly accursed: he is still to be denied, it seems, that longed-for epiphany of the printed word. He shakes his head and bemoans the selfish act that has placed him in this humiliating position:

'If only I hadn't been so bolshie in that charity shop. When I found that £5,000 book priced at 50p, and the volunteer suggested I'd got a bit of a bargain there, would I like to make a little extra contribution? And I declined, the book was marked at 50p, I said, why should I pay more than that, famine or no famine? Oh it was mean of me, a ten-thousandfold profit, and as a result I must spend as many days in this tedious waiting-room, starved of so much as a magazine, and only myself to blame.'

Decades more elapse in this tantalising state, until our friend is ready to ascend the next rung of the ladder. Here at last he gets to see the printed word for the first time. Finding himself opposite a shelf of detective stories in paperback, he picks up the first one. Imagine his delight as he beholds real type! He launches into a narrative, a very badly written one, but a story nonetheless, with characters and a plot, with a beginning, a middle and a ... Well, perhaps it was too much to ask, he should have known he hadn't been spared yet, for the story never reaches its conclusion. Just as the detective has assembled all the suspects in the room for the dénouement, and the name of the guilty party is on his lips... the book peters out in a series of dots. Clearly these are special editions printed for the use of purgatory victims like himself, one might almost say rare books in their way, but of no practical use in this location. And so he moves on, from one interminable rung to another, to the accompaniment of bland hotel lift music, so inoffensive it positively offends.

Progress is minimal. For instance, the next rung brings him to a shelf of complete books—ah yes, but just look at them. A technical book on the industrial use of polymers, a novelette in Portuguese, the two-volume *Dictionary of National Biography* (minus, however, the magnifying glass), a manual for BetaMax video recorders, yes, every one a loser, each one a proud purveyor of useless information, hardly fodder for the curious mind. And speaking of Fodor, there are plenty of out-of-date travel guides just for good measure, inviting him to savour the undiminished splendours of the church of St Francis of Assisi, or the peace and harmony of the port of Dubrovnik.

His appetite for books is almost ruined; almost but not quite. For he is a collector, a bibliophile, an academic, or just plain dealer who has spent his whole life in the pursuit of knowledge—why should death change him? You probably noticed that the word 'dealer' came last on my list of purgatorial sufferers. I'm convinced, you see, that the majority of this breed, those who have no interest in books outside their commercial value, go straight to hell. Naturally I let myself off the hook. For one thing, this is my afterlife, so I'll take up residence where I choose (quite frankly, I think hell would be the death of me). And besides, it's a matter of logistics: if I was stuck down there, how would I be able to get a peep at purgatory, let alone heaven, and describe it for you?

Having had more than his fill of indigestible book fodder, eventually our friend climbs onto the next rung, the mediocre, and the next, the vaguely interesting, all the time gradually shedding pounds of sins. He becomes lighter and lighter, his progress from rung to rung quickens, it's not decades now but lustrums, then a matter of years, months, days, his momentum increases like an athlete's, until finally he reaches the top rung of the ladder.

Now he stands opposite a wall of very nice books indeed, though look a little closer and you'll see that even here the dust-jackets are chipped, or the cloth is a little bubbled, some minor imperfection remains even on this highest of shelves. But he reads each one with pleasure. And our friend has become so light that every time he leans over to pick out a new book he feels giddy. He comes to the last one: it engrosses him, it even contains a reference to himself, alluding to his failed attempt to put it back on the shelf. Life mirrors art, it seems—well, after-life. As he stretches out his arm to do so, he loses his footing, slips off the ladder, and becomes light as air, breasting the current, floating up through the hatch in the ceiling, and on into an attic-like darkness, till his surroundings brighten, he bobs up into a blaze of heavenly light, to the buoyant melody of the opening prelude of Bach's *Well-Tempered Clavier*, still clutching the book, the one that uplifted him for his final journey, encapsulating the mysteries of worshipful bookfulness. (Oh no, not again, you will say—and oh yes, I must reply; but before you accuse me of conceit, let me say that I consider it *a* conceit, and nothing more.)

Yes, his eyes must adjust not only to the golden-toned light of his new dwelling, but its vast dimensions. In whatever direction he turns the perspective appears to be immeasurable, expanding outwards, ever-lengthening beyond his field of vision. Yet, paradoxically, he has the definite impression of a room, enclosed by fortress-like walls, lined for miles and miles with mahogany shelves, whose resinous wood-smoke mingles with the ambrosial odour of freshly polished bindings. He floats up and down on his cloud of pleasure, noting above him a skylight through which, presumably, the golden light is pouring, and yet no matter how high he ascends he never reaches the roof, it seems to recede further and further away. He finds it hard to adjust to the scale of his new surroundings, temporal as well as spatial, for he might have been here minutes or centuries, already he has known such boundless pleasure he can scarcely endure it. And yet he knows it is eternal.

As he looks about him with wonder, he sees other beings like himself floating about, book beings certainly, but neither braying of conquests, nor consumed with remorse for past peccadilloes; on the contrary, they are drifting through the ether in ecstasy. And though the air space is filled with thousands of these beings, he never gets close to them, even when he seems to be on collision course with someone there is never any contact. It is as if they are regulated by air traffic control; he is convinced that in the empyrean someone is monitoring their movements. Uncluttered by pollution, the air is a crystal clear current, carrying merely that waft of healthy book odour with which he fills his lungs.

Floating towards these endless galleries of books, he picks out a shelf at random, and homes in on... he can hardly believe his eyes! Not only is it *Paradise Lost*, first edition, 1667, but it's in mint condition, it's never been opened, or if it has, and surely in this company it must have been, it *looks* untouched. Soon he discovers that in heaven all books remain in their original state; because there are no germs here, no sweat, these purified hands can't sully the paper, nor with their weightlessness can they damage the binding. He lifts up the Milton, and takes it with him, and in doing so he drops *Second-Hand Books: a First-Hand View* (OK, OK, I know my place), which latter falls through the hatch and occupies its previous place as the last book one sees before leaving purgatory, the ultimate cream cleanser of the soul. He is surprised how light it is to carry, but even the elephant folios have a different weight in this gravity-defying atmosphere. As there is no furniture here, he wonders how he is to read it, but he simply experiments, and finds he can peruse with perfect ease while lying prone on the air, supine, or just plain sitting down—the air is suitably cushioned for the heavenly bottom. Nor does he ever have to get up to have a meal, for the only food here is the mental consumption of books, and without cause there is no effect, he can read for hours, years at a time, untroubled by physical urges. He reads with perfect concentration, such as he has never known before, there are no distractions, the bodies flying past him make no sound, indeed they fan the air slightly, there is always a pleasing breeze to complement the permanently mild weather. And though these include female bodies (talk about heavenly bottoms!), no, the only kind of lust is for knowledge, and not the carnal variety.

The music comes from God knows where, but whatever the source it must be state-of-the-art technology, for it's the best CD sound system he's ever heard. Every detail is transparently clear, he can't remember hearing Bach's 48 played with such spiritual insight, nor Messiaen's *Le Verbe*, nor Tallis' *Spem in Alium*, and always the most soul-expanding music, never a hint of the cheap or meretricious. It appears that God is not only an air traffic controller but a disc jockey as well; every now and then our friend notices scraps of paper floating past his head on their journey up towards the Almighty. But certain requests are ignored—not all of them meet the rigorous requirements, some are actually for popular music, Billie Holiday or even Blur, and these He won't play. (Well, our dwellers are here for their love of books; one can't expect them to have ideal musical taste to boot!) A creative genius Himself, God is bound to be a little choosy.

As he familiarises himself with his new environment, he realises that the books are arranged in chronological order. There is a vast section of illuminated manuscripts, shelf after shelf of incunabula, many of which he has never heard of let alone seen, including a pristine Gutenberg Bible—just as well, he thinks, there are no thieves in heaven. All are in their original parchment or vellum, fresh from the monks' quill or off the earliest printing presses, Caxtons and Aldines, assembled with the meticulous care, the love of knowledge, and above all the sense of its importance, that had to be lavished on this single means of communication open to these craftsmen. In our age of convenience and multi-media, we have inevitably become blasé, we tend to spurn the primitive methods of an earlier time.

Every influential book from every period is here. More's *Utopia*, Machiavelli's *The Prince*, Geneva Bibles, Henry VIII's *Defence of Faith*, and then on into the age of Shakespeare, a First Folio of course, *Don Quixote*, Hobbes' *Leviathan*, Milton and the Metaphysicals, *Pilgrim's Progress* (a complete copy, signed but not singed), Locke's *Essay* and the Age of Enlightenment, sets of Pope and Swift, Adam Smith's *Wealth of Nations*, the *Lyrical Ballads*, sets of Jane Austen, Dickens and the Brontës, editions of Darwin and Wallace, Marx, Freud and Einstein, the modernist peaks of *The Waste Land* and *Ulysses*, then on into our own illustrious age and...

Trainspotting?

Oh well, perhaps every period looks on itself with despair, maybe the readers of Wordsworth and Coleridge thought this was dross compared to Shakespeare, the audience of the Bard harked back to the Graeco-Roman classics, the Greeks... now there's a thought, where did they go for nostalgia? In the great span of future history who knows but that *Trainspotting* might become a landmark by which all other books are measured. Actually I've never read it—partly because I never read books in a foreign language—but I know many people who swear by it. Whatever one's taste, eternity itself would scarcely be enough time to read all the volumes here, so vast is our heritage, so rich and multifarious. Mind you, that depends of course on how long that eternity is, I mean, are we talking short-term or long-term? But even if it's a real whacking great eternity (it's no use, it's always finite in our living imagination), new books are being printed all the time, books of the future (or is that a misnomer?), none of the readers here will ever get through them all. So there is no complacency in this book-lover's heaven, there is always another volume donated by God to fathom out, forever that burning curiosity which motivates the voracious reader.

And always the perfect setting, free from the intrusions of platitudinous chit-chat, of street noise, of machine. Only that divine musical background, exterior sound mirroring interior thought, and all aspiring towards the figure enthroned at the very top under the skylight, swathed in cloud. Glimpses of Him, however, are occasionally granted, and now the curtains of clouds part to reveal... wait a minute, why if He isn't (He can't be) standing on a rostrum... *conducting*. But it's more than that, it's not just God wielding a baton, there are angels on either side, one phalanx an orchestra, the other a choir. Of course, this is no mere CD system, this is a live performance, no wonder it's so divine, it's from the hand of the Maestro Himself. Such magnificent ensemble! And it's not simply the music He's conducting, not just the *Ode to Joy* blasting through the boundless magnificence of this aerated room, but everything else that goes on in the room too, in all rooms, between us and books, the permanent interaction between writer and reader that has existed down the centuries from one corner of the earth to another, back to the beginnings of literacy itself. Yes, in the beginning was the Word all right, and the word was... (well, if you don't know by now)... yes, my magnificent reader, the word was BOOK.

14

Book Sales

After floating around in eternity for an hour or so, it is time to come crashing down to reality once more with an almighty thump. Be warned: you are in dangerous waters: for you have joined me just as I am queueing up to enter (I can hardly say it) the charity book sale.

> 'The Charity Book Sale! Hardly are those words out
> Than a vast image out of *Spiritus Mundi*
> Troubles my sight...'

Put it this way, if Yeats had ever been to one of these occasions he might well have chosen it as a prime example of how Christian values have been subverted.

Like bazaars and jumbles, these book sales are held in churches, schools and community centres throughout the capital on behalf of Amnesty International or Christian Aid or a political party or institution. They are not to be confused with book *fairs*; superficially at least, they are not run by or for the trade. They may enlist the aid of a local dealer, and indeed I suspect that many of these sales are creamed off beforehand, at least judging by the quality of the merchandise left behind. But good, bad or ugly, the books are a lot cheaper than they would be in a shop, sometimes as little as 20p or 50p for a paperback, and £1 for hardbacks. In the current second-hand book climate, with the ever-increasing dissemination of knowledge to an ever larger number of people, bargains are hard to find, and such sales can seem an attractive proposition. On paper. The trouble is, there are as many dealers present as ordinary members of the reading public, sometimes more. The latter have neither the time nor the mercenary incentive to attend; on the whole they prefer to browse at leisure in a bookshop. And any of them who are unlucky enough to stray into such a battle zone once, may well be put off from ever doing so again. For where there is money to be made, you will see men (and women) behaving badly.

Who are these dealers? People like myself with a large shop to feed; those who run a stall in a market or students' union; collectors who part-fund their bibliomania by selling a few books on the side; academics, runners, the Mr Singhs of this world. We have only one thing in common: we are all small fry. Serious booksellers, second-hand or antiquarian, do not attend: they deal, in short, in proper books, the sort I described in heaven. What you find in these sales is rarely in that category, more in the upper (and lower) reaches of purgatory. But they are cheap. And once you've been doing this for a while, you get to know the sales to avoid, as well as the better ones (though these can vary in quality from year to year).

While some of the books may be publishers' throw-outs, damaged stock or future remainders, the majority are handed in by the general public, collected by local scouts doing the rounds. These books have been donated either by the owners themselves, who can't be bothered to go through the ordinary selling process (for reasons I made clear earlier), or by surviving relatives. The result of a sale can often depend on one contribution: many is the time I've come across a load of old rubbish, but in one corner I've found, it may be, several items about arms and armour, including a three-volume history of the revolver—there's that much to say?—all with the same owner's inscription.

It is unfortunate, but people are very interested in guns; one shouldn't encourage this perhaps, but they are. And there are other subjects I'm reluctant to buy. Books on hunting, for instance, which attract the kind of country folk who reinforce my preference for animals over human beings; or the occult, which brings in a variety of oddballs—from the comparatively harmless Gothic (pale, cadaverous, swathed in Draculoid cloaks) to the seriously loony Crowley acolyte, resonant of rape and bloody sacrifice. Then again, there's fascism. Here's an ideology which includes book-burning and the eradication of free speech, but am I not in danger of becoming a fascist myself (worse, a hypocrite) if I then refuse to sell their ideology, forbid their voice to be heard? Get too fastidious, and you could end up buying (and selling) absolutely nothing. Take an ordinary antique price guide: this is very useful to a dealer or collector, and generally is bought by such; but it will also be sought by a thief who has just lifted a piece of Sèvres, and needs to know its value.

Now let's go back to the queue. In order to get anything at these book sales it's a good idea to be one of the front runners. It is Sod's Law that if I queue a half-hour early, in all kinds of weather, the sale will open on time, or even a few minutes late; if for any reason I happen to be delayed, and get there with only five minutes to spare, the queue will already be going in, leaving me at an even greater disadvantage. At most of these sales the dealers arrive one after another, more or less at the front of the queue, and start chatting in a cluster. Well, most of us do. Relations between us are governed by an uneasy kind of camaraderie; it is far from fake, indeed for many of us it is almost a social occasion, there is no point in serious acrimony. True, the climate changes when we go in—we are suddenly rivals—but providing nobody breaks the unwritten rules, when we meet up again we'll be amicably chatting once more. Naturally there are feuds, but I'm not at liberty to discuss them: x and y, for instance, simply will not speak to each other, to the extent that if they do need to communicate they enlist the aid of z (i.e. me) as conversational go-between. But if I were to describe it here in detail, perhaps x and y would join forces, and cold-shoulder me instead.

I mentioned rules just now. Clearly if there are six or seven dealers chasing only a few decent books in a confined space, there is the potential for trouble, and people will be guilty of pushing and shoving, getting in one another's way. (Oddly enough, the worst offenders are the 'Cookheads', little old ladies lunging after Catherine Cooksons: never mind the frailty, feel the elbow.) But there is no excuse for standing rigidly over a whole section of the table, with arms akimbo, and not letting anyone else get a hand, let alone a look-in. It is possible to position yourself where you want to be and still allow people in on either side of you. I am sure I have been a nuisance, but I have never blocked anyone *deliberately*. I am a great believer in fair play, and when I see it abused I get very angry indeed.

Take queue-jumpers. There are those who work their way up from the back of a queue, heads down, millipede-slow, creeping up ever so gradually, past one, past another, hoping they won't be noticed, and apparently oblivious to their own actions when they are caught *in flagrante*. Others are even more shameless. I remember a huge queue at one sale, and this woman arriving at the last minute who simply walks down the line past everybody, past scores and scores of rain-bedraggled mortals, and takes up her position in front of the first man—so casually, too, so naturally, it hardly occurs to anyone to question the move. Oh well, perhaps the chap in front was keeping her place. Uh-uh— I asked him: he'd never seen her before in his life. She simply couldn't be bothered to queue like everybody else, and she was so brazen she got away with it.

Queue-jumping, however, is one thing; queue-*jamming* is quite another. On one occasion I was next in line behind a dealer who had brought along a friend, or in this case I should say an accomplice, a particularly large one. He resembled Yeats' 'rough beast', only instead of having a 'lion body' it was more the thick padded bulk of a rhino. I'm calculating that with only this one creature between us, the dealer has perhaps a five-second advantage over me (unfortunately such detail matters). As the time approaches, we psych ourselves up, the adrenalin starts to pump. The man on the door is ready, he starts taking the 20p entrance fee, the dealer drops his change into the outstretched palm and rushes through the narrow doorway, then the friend steps up to pay, jingling myriad coppers in his hand. But as he sticks out his massive paw, he fumbles at the last moment, the coins go scattering clangorously all over the floor, he starts picking them up, one by one, penny by penny, with excruciating slowness—I am going spare—till finally he rights himself with a crick, and counts the money out (ever-so-helpfully) into the outstretched palm, all the time blocking the doorway with his enormous stature. Alas this second coming personified is not into 'slouching'—if I could have wriggled past him, I would have done. So that by the time rhino is moving his 'slow thighs' and I have gone careering past him up onto the dais where the books are, I have lost a vital thirty seconds or so, and my rival has a pile (oh yes, quite possible in such a short period of time) of twenty books.

You could say I'm being paranoid, his friend just happened to be huge and clumsy, and I would concede there must be a 10 per cent chance that you are right. But I doubt it. I have antennae, and as far as I'm concerned, it was an elaborately prepared ploy. I suppose I ought to be flattered; I posed such a threat I had to be delayed. Nevertheless it's the sort of flattery I can do without. This has not led to a feud: partly because of a lingering doubt, partly because the execution was superb. Yes, I always admire good technique, even when harnessed to an invidious action. If I no longer trust this dealer, I have occasionally exchanged words with him, there is an attempt at civility. Don't think I'm blowing my own trumpet: on the contrary, by muting my resentment I've allowed it to fester. Maybe I should return the favour, bring along my own fat, and decidedly accident-prone, friend.

But this experience was nothing compared to another incident that took place. You will notice that so far I have not used any names in this book; it is not and never has been my intention to score points off any rivals, to tread on any... hooves (of the cloven variety). No, I am not childish, not bitter and twisted, all these people shall remain anonymous—even Declan. Whoops! Oh dear, it just slipped out, sorry about that; well, now that it's there, let me tell you something about Declan. Oddly enough, I can think of far worse things that have been done to me; but it wasn't so much *what* he did as *how*. I am pleased to say this was the only occasion I clashed swords with him, for he has now disappeared. Whether he has moved to a different area or out of the book trade altogether I do not know, but I would not be surprised (even less dismayed) to learn that he has been detained at Her Majesty's pleasure, or 'taken out' by contract killing—for others, too, have suffered at his hands.

We get the idea, I hear you clamouring, so what did Declan actually do?

In the mad scramble for books there is usually a split second in which to make a successful grab at something or thereafter regret it. The eye-to-brain-to-hand coordination involves quick reflexes, sometimes too quick, resulting in wrong connections, picking up books you don't especially want. And the irony of this whole business was that the book which I grabbed was not very interesting, an ordinary volume of naval history, worth £10 at best. In the natural course of things I might even have put it back later... if it had been mine to put back, that is.

So I've just put out my hand to secure this book, and lo and behold, if another hand doesn't reach out from the other side of the table and latch onto it as well, a full second after me, no more than that, but in these circumstances a second, believe me, is decisive. The book is mine then, I got to it first, I know that, he knows that, there's nothing to discuss. Naturally, because I got to it first, I'm still holding onto it, but less naturally, though he got to it second, Declan is doing the same, and so we are standing there, hands locked over this book, apparently frozen in time.

It's no use, I won't speak, for if I speak I will spit, I think instead of people I have lost over the years, in the hope that I can summon up a look that will be enough, a look which begs the question: 'why should a horse, a dog, a *rat* have life...?' I give him the loudest look of which I am capable, I stare at this facsimile of a human being, and what is he doing? He is not only staring straight back at me, there is an incipient tremor, his lips curl ever so slightly into a smile. He is telling me, also without words, for he can't possibly argue his case, that he knows I got there first, but he is going to have the book anyway, because he is Declan, he is going to stand there for hours, days, *months* if need be, and never let go of it. By now I'm in toxic shock—and he knows, does Declan, that short of making an almighty row, which will only be my word against his, there is nothing I can do, except be as persistent as he is. Out of the question! I won't be contaminated by his shamelessness. Ten seconds is all it takes: such a brief stand-off in real terms, and yet I have never forgotten those atoms of time. Like me, Declan probably didn't even need the book, saw no great value in it; he wanted it, I suspect, more because I had beaten him to it, like an insufferable brat that can't keep its hands off someone else's possessions.

Yes, I let the book go, for all the reasons I just mentioned, but also, genuinely, because I started to get frightened. I felt that if I had to confront that runtish, dishonest smile any longer, I might not be responsible for my actions. The story of Billy Budd came to mind, how one can just run up against a person who is an embodiment of injustice (to call Declan a devil would be to flatter him—the devil is not cheap). I am not an aggressive man, some would say quite the opposite, but if ever in my life I could have hurt someone that was the moment. Unlike the punch of Billy Budd, however, I can't pretend mine would have been fatal—no, and maybe *that's* the reason I didn't use it.

Declan is, or hopefully was, in a class of his own: compared to him, we are all amateurs. In case you think I can only dish out the dirt and don't like it when the wind carries it back in my face (does anyone like this?), let me say that no one can participate in such open combat, year in year out, without having his reputation tarnished. What do they say of me? I doubt if I know the half of it, but in the crossfire I have overheard nicknames. In some quarters I believe I am known as the 'octopus'—and it's true that my hands do shoot off in all directions with a certain elasticity. I confess I quite like the term; though not intended as a compliment, I take it as one. True, an octopus is not a thing of beauty, but then, nor am I.

It doesn't end there though. Another man who didn't know my methods unnerved me once with a direct question.

'When it comes to books, are you a sniper or a mass murderer?'

Confessing that I was more in the Charles Manson line of business, he nodded, as if to say, 'thought as much'. And there

I've hit on my chief source of offence. For the great majority are snipers, not just members of the public, but dealers too. They have a speciality, or up to two or three subjects that they know well: for one it might be science and natural history, for another literature and philosophy. I work in a general bookshop that deals in most categories, so I buy across the board. I will frequently stray into other people's specialised areas, and this will inevitably cause annoyance. My knowledge on the subject of cookery may well be inferior to someone who only deals in this, but it's good enough at this level, and if I'm quicker on the draw...

Yes, being a mass murderer does seem to gall a lot of people. Coming away with only one or two bodies themselves, they will buzz around my huge pile of corpses, and gawp. Especially those who are not familiar with me. 'Are you taking all of these?' Well, yes, and why not? They talk to me as if they really are corpses, or at the very least, books I've stolen. It's as if I'm not *allowed* to buy so much. (Indeed at an animals' benefit I attended, the person in charge got quite stroppy. 'You're not leaving enough for anybody else,' he said. Choosing to ignore this nonsense, I went on quietly selecting till he really showed his fangs. 'STOP-RIGHT-THERE!!!' he raged at me. And I had thought the idea was to *save* the tiger, not become one.) But I've queued with the best of them, sometimes for as long as an hour in wind and rain, and all I've done is gone in and used my knowledge. Casual punters remain so incredulous, so indignant over my haul that when my back is turned and I'm looking out for a taxi, they come and grab something off my pile (talk about snipers) and are almost walking off with it before I notice. When I inform them that the book is mine, yes, paid for, they actually sneer and take offence.

In a way I can understand why ordinary readers have an aversion to dealers: whereas they just want to enjoy the book, I'm doing it for business. So occasionally I let them have something. Big mistake: give them an inch...

'Excuse me, do you think you could let me have that Joanna Trollope? I wouldn't ask, only I've been after it for ages. Thank you: you *are* kind. But what's this? *The Canterbury Tales*! Do you know, that's on my daughter's reading list? Yes... sorry to... that really is the last one. Only—would you believe it?—*Maldoror*, my nephew's boyfriend wants to—'

Sod her nephew: I'm doing her a favour. For all I know, she might even be a dealer in disguise. No, it doesn't do to be kind: it brings out the very worst in people.

Readers are one thing, and ninety-nine times out of a hundred, they do just want to read the book. I respect that. Unfortunately there is another species with an aversion to dealers, one whose supercilious contempt for our ranks is apparently in inverse proportion to their reliance on our spending power. I refer to that phenomenon that goes by the name of 'helper'. I ought to explain that, to a dealer, the word 'helper' is as hateful as vice versa. This is not a good start, I admit, but bad experiences on both sides, over the chequered history of charity book sales, have left this residue of mutual distrust, like a political stalemate with irreconcilable differences. It is not true of all situations; there are plenty of sales where relations between the two are perfectly cordial. I have known positive, alert, unbiased helpers who have done just what is required of them (that is, supervising a stall, taking money, and seeing that fair play is conducted). Still this is an entertainment, or is designed to be; and just as a documentary will focus on the dark side of an institution, and not on more everyday dealings, so I must do the same here. A significant minority, then, are a disgrace to their name: far from helping, they are more of a hindrance. My view is not entirely one-sided though. Doubtless helpers could tell a few stories about us, and I've taken that into consideration, as you will see if you read on. I say 'if', for readers with a distaste for graphic violence with a bit of blasphemy thrown in, may wish to skip the rest of this chapter.[1]

---

[1] Now if that isn't guaranteed to make you read on...

BOOK SALES

Are you with me? Right then. Given the competitive nature of most book sales, it is often time-consuming to check over the books one has grabbed, and they become so heavy it is necessary to put the accumulated pile down. The only safe place is behind the table in the helpers' domain. But when you've finished, some will not let you go through your pile, even at a quick glance, to put back any books that are damaged (and many of them are—that is why they are there). In a cheap book sale this hardly matters; but sometimes you are paying £3 or more for each book, and if half of them should have been invalided out, this can add up to an expensive series of mistakes.

You may echo the sentiments of the dear helper by suggesting I should have checked before. Easier said than done. Not only would I be wasting precious time, allowing my rivals to pounce on five books in a matter of seconds; sometimes it is not even physically possible, one is involved in a scrimmage, barged by people on all sides, and standing still amidst such a maelstrom is positively dangerous. Maybe this is our lookout, and as long as the price is written inside, or colour-coded by means of a sticky label—in itself enough to damage the book when you peel it off—fair enough. But sometimes prices are utterly random, they seem to make them up as they go along; and if a book turns out to be expensive, not only are you not allowed to check it through again, you're subjected to a lecture to boot, how you've got yourself a real bargain. Oh yes, with a cigarette burn in the middle of the cover, a coffee stain down the fore-edge, and a whopping great bogey sticking together pages six and seven. They seem to think they know more about books than you do; they're worse than customers.

Being vague about the price is one thing; far worse if they have a system—50p for paperbacks, £1 for hardbacks—and then proceed to make... adjustments.

'I thought you said the paperbacks were 50p.'
'No no, you misunderstood me. It's 50p for the smaller ones; the fatter ones are £1.'
'But you didn't say that.'

BOOK SALES

'I'm saying it now.'

So then you have to work through a pile of a hundred paperbacks, separating out all the fat ones. But when does a thin one become a fat one? Some are easy enough to distinguish, it is true: one is generally safe with a minimalist like Beckett, and penalised for a chatterer like Thackeray. But what about medium-length books? Come on, you can guess: that's right: they're 75p. Not only do I now face the prospect of three piles, I must put up with the helpers' shambolic powers of addition. Three doses of it. (Or is that four?) And woe betide you should you attempt to quicken matters by helping the helper to add up; clearly you are trying to show them up, worse, swindle them. No, the only thing to do at such sales is to head exclusively for the thin books—it saves both time and trouble.

There is some preconceived idea in these people's minds that the more paper a book uses, the more valuable it must be; they make the same distinction between the newer and glossier titles, with great fat modern price-tags on them, and the older, grubbier publications at 8/6 (which come in at 20p—their idea of half-price). I'm ashamed to admit it took even me some time to get out of the habit of always going for the larger, shinier books, partly because their prominence attracts the eye (like pom-pom chrysanthemums), and to develop infrared vision for the shrinking violet of a dusty pamphlet—how about Virginia Woolf's little essay on Sickert, not many pages certainly, but worth close on £100.

Sometimes, however, the only desirable items *are* the fat ones, and then I'm in trouble. I feel like saying:

'Look, you're a thin person, one might even say anorexic, does this mean you're less important, less valuable than Friar Tuck over there?' (pointing at the vicar).

Some helpers have such a 'thing' about me that I feel like I'm in the dock.

'Are you a paedophile?' one of them asked me once.

Actually the word she had used was 'dealer', but the tone, I swear, was 'paedophile'. Then all the stakes are suddenly raised:

all the books that are £1 to everyone else (or less—members of the public often get a discount for buying a few measly romances) are now £2 to me. If I'm spending as much as £50 it must be because the firm is going to make a profit out of them, and they can't bear that, so suddenly I'm spending £100, and still I'm an outcast. It amounts to a mathematical equation: dealer = scumbag².[2]

At one sale I went to, we were all assigned 'minders'. I went in, started picking up books here and there, and within seconds I got the impression I was being hounded, in itself not unusual, but in this case I was literally being shadowed by a man with a bag. Now helpful as it is to have your hands free, your burden removed, it is extremely *un*helpful to have someone breathing down your neck. It is also abundantly obvious—from the running commentary provided by the person in charge—that their main motive is to ensure you don't put anything into *your* bag.

> 'Watch that one; watch him like a hawk. Keep up, man, he's getting away from you. And you there—this is your first time, isn't it?—well, wipe that smirk off your face and mark baldie in the corner. He caused a right little fracas last year; in the end I had to bring him down with a rugby tackle. No no, I didn't say get ahead of him—can't you see you're offside?'

The truth is, dealers are like everyone else: some are sneaky, make a fuss, try and have everything their own way; others are honest, pay up quickly, and do it with a good grace. You shouldn't automatically assume the worst; nor should you charge one price to one person, and double it for another. It is unfair, and for all I know, illegal. Certainly if a bookseller tried to do that ... You can always refuse to sell a book (I know of

---

[2]Which, in booksellers' parlance, reads: 'dealer = folio-sized scumbag'

someone who went as far as ripping one up rather than letting a difficult customer have it), but that's all. A charity may be different, but at the very least it should be... well, charitable. Especially if it has religious affiliations.

Some of the worst helpers in my experience are Catholics. By this I don't mean ordinary run-of-the-mill Catholics, but those of a higher caste, snooty upper-class cliques, the ones who will only attend 'marss' if it's in Latin, who are more concerned with hieratic paraphernalia than Christian virtues. And it is not the priest or monsignor or what's-his-name who is guilty; no no, they are usually far too jolly or ineffectual. Or just jolly ineffectual. It is his henchmen, members of the congregation, collecting money for the restoration fund. These people love their church so much they are the sworn enemies of humanity. It is not just that they filter out all the best books beforehand to some chosen dealer, and doubtless some more into their own pockets (to adapt a popular phrase: 'God helps those helpers who help themselves'); they then charge extortionate prices for the humble items that remain, and proceed to...

Imagine a beautiful June day, a marquee that has been erected for a midsummer fête, and inside some fifteen tables of books, each manned by at least one helper, sometimes two. I go in, I arrive at the first table, I pick out a few books, and then, naturally, I would like to move on to the second table (other dealers are swarming all over the place), but before I can do this someone barks in my face, 'Where are you going with those?' I explain that I would like a preliminary scout about, and I am then informed that I have to pay first. 'At each table?' I protest. Apparently so. It is only after the clearest possible argument, that such a process could take hours, that I intend to spend a lot but can only do this if I have a free run at everything—i.e. leave books aside and then pay at the end—that I eventually reach a compromise. Considerably delayed, I move on, but I get the same flak at the next table, and the next. I feel like Daniel in the lions' den, desperately I look around for someone sensible to intercede for me, there's no sign of the Virgin so I head for a lesser one, the priest, and some sort of sanity is restored.

But it isn't over yet. This is merely the scourging: hammer

and nails come later. For I have yet to pay for the books. Are they going to make it easy for me? Are they hell! I omit the possibility that some of my books may have been mixed up with someone else's, others have been put back because I haven't reclaimed them quickly enough, and as for checking the condition of any of them... no, these points I won't mention. So now I have books at maybe ten tables, and what do I find? Each helper expects me to pay separately. No doubt they are all in competition with each other ('Well, our table took £75, so boo-hoo to you!'), forgetting that all the takings go to the church anyway, and not to them. I try to explain that I pay by company cheque, and it is a little galling to be expected to use ten of these, especially when some of the amounts are under £5. They look at me suspiciously, as if I'm trying to wriggle out of payment altogether, and once again I find myself turning to the priest, it's almost like confession:

'Father, I have this problem.'
'Is it self-abuse, my son?'
'No, it is the abuse of others, your confederates, in fact.'
'Say ten Hail Marys and six Our Fathers.'
'But *they're* abusing *me!*'
'Say five Hail Marys and three Our Fathers.'
'Is that all you can say?'
'I'm a priest, goddammit, whose side do you think I'm on?'

After much negotiation, I gather together all the different piles from all the different tables, and get them into one place. By this stage I don't even care what I'm lumbered with, I just want to get out of there as quickly as possible—back to civilisation. All right, the shop. I may have done a good morning's business, but it's taken years off my life.

Sometimes it is not the helpers who are the problem, so much as the venue. The room in which they have chosen to hold the book sale is too narrow for the three-ring circus about to take place. Or the table is too small to contain all the books that have been donated, so now there are cartons of unsorted books underneath, adding chaos at floor level to the mayhem above. Or the books are double-parked, one long row of paperbacks concealed behind another. There is one notorious venue in Blackheath, a church, where the books are not displayed on tables so much as arranged along the pews. Now I'm not an expert in ecclesiastical matters, or at least I only go to church when a book sale is on, but damn my heathen soul if they're not the narrowest pews in England.

Picture a crowd of dealers (none too photogenic) queueing hungrily one morning, hammering at the entrance, the doors burst open, 'mere anarchy is loosed upon the world', and scudding in on a 'blood-dimmed tide' comes an onrush of slavering book crazies. Eyes starting out of his head, the creature at the front scampers up the first pew he comes to, finds nothing he wants, panics, goes into reverse, scampers back down, but he runs into an oncoming rival, they are trapped, there is no room to manoeuvre, only with a scratching and a scraping do they finally manage to squeeze past each other. Meanwhile other dealers are frantically taking up positions in other pews, there is much reaching over and under and around, a dealer stuck in one pew spots an interesting book in the next, he leans over the wooden bench to make a grab for it, but another dealer in the right place sees where he's aiming and whisks it away in front of him. Someone else crouching on all fours to look at a box beneath a pew suddenly finds himself flattened like a hedgehog, struggling for breath; a demon is climbing on his back to get at a book he can't otherwise reach above this human footstool. In the transept to the right another is zealously scooping up paperbacks by the dozen, but the burden, held against his chest, is toppling, there is nowhere safe to put it down, he goes on piling and piling until the whole edifice crumbles like a pack of cards. Books go flying everywhere, and before he knows it all about him 'reel shadows of the indignant desert birds', other dealers come scavenging around the carrion, scuffles break out between old enemies, perhaps new ones are made, for 'the best lack all conviction, and the worst /Are full of passionate intensity'. Stunned, he stands there, clutching at nothing now; and, bombarded from all sides, starts spinning like a top. All this is happening at breakneck pace within sight of the Saviour, who stares down woefully from his crucifix, wondering why his 'ceremony of innocence' has been drowned in such monstrous behaviour. 'Things fall apart' (a table collapses), 'the centre cannot hold' (a book is torn in two after a tug-of-war), and it isn't long before 'the darkness drops again' (several candelabra have been overturned), and the 'stony sleep' of this quiet church, not to mention peaceful neighbourhood, is 'vexed to nightmare' by our pack of baying hounds.

This is the book sale from the helper's point of view. It is understandable, then, after such an inglorious vision of humanity, why they carry away such a negative impression of the book trade. (Ironically enough, the helpers at this particular sale are thoroughly good-natured, almost too tolerant in fact. Perhaps it is only when one side plays the game impeccably that the other commits a series of bookable offences.)

Of course, these are extreme cases; it isn't normally so bad, or I wouldn't go back. There are many things on the plus side too. Partly, I suspect, it is the human diversity that draws me. And the occasional bargain. In any case I would prefer to be in the thick of the action than to be sitting in the shop with no customers for the same length of time. More often than not, I emerge unscathed, at worst there is minor bruising, a pulled muscle. Though I expect nothing, there is always the hope; on balance, I am pleasantly surprised as often as bitterly disappointed. Success often depends on knowing the lie of the land: where each category in the room is placed—art on the left at the front, biography to the right at the back—what sort of books this sale tends to have, and at what price. There's one held in a church hall which is even more clear-cut: it has windows on the near side instead of a wall, which means that while queueing I can pick out in advance all the books I'm going to make for, instead of frantically searching once inside.

I rarely do well at a venue of unknown territory. When the doors open I don't know where to head for first, I tend to waste time getting my bearings. Occasionally you hear stories of dealers picking off the best book thirty minutes into a sale, and I myself have been lucky on going around for the umpteenth time, homing in on something another dealer has put back. Generally, however, it's over in minutes, and only the same old reliables remain. For when six months or a year go by, and it is time for the next sale, these perennials that you hoped never to see again are brought out from storage once more to see the prosaic light of day. Even dustier, mustier than before. Their leaves expand for a few hours, but when it is over they will inevitably be packed away in the same dark vault, sitting out another year, and then another.

These books are finished, and should be treated as such. Sometimes they are passed on to charity shops, and will take up residence there for another decade, unless some volunteer thinks there's a limit to sentiment, and sends them off to be pulped for a few pennies. Books, like people, are mortal, and badly produced or seriously dated ones will have a shorter life than most. When they have served their purpose—or, equally, outstayed their welcome—who says euthanasia is wrong? I am not encouraging any private person out there to lethally inject his library—far from it. Give your unwanted books to charity, and the natural process will work itself out.

Which reminds me of some *un*natural practices. Recently the appalling business with Frank Kermode, part of whose priceless collection of first editions and original manuscripts got shredded in a mix-up between garbage and removal men. I myself once talked to a house clearance bloke who claimed to have found 'filthy old science books past their sell-by date, covers hanging off, with loads of piccies of out-of-date gizmos inside'; without thinking, he threw them on the city dump.

'How old?' I asked with some trepidation.
'Dunno. It was all in Roaming numerals. Something about MCC.'
Roaming indeed.
'This isn't cricket, you know.'

I felt sick. Eighteenth-century engravings of industrial

technology worth hundreds of pounds! In the long run I suppose the great majority of books come to an unfortunate end, much the same as their owners. Perhaps the paper of one knackered book went into the making of this one; I shudder to think what may happen to my own.

Go, little book...

15

The Future of The Book

[The year is circa 2050. A middle-class home. An endless procession of hardware and software, ROM-ing and RAM-ing, microfiche and microchips. Even the dog is called Micro. Where is culture? That's it. 'Ware' is culture. The only glimmer of hope is a stack of books on a table; there are others, too, sorted into piles on the floor. What follows is a conversation between Cathy, a girl of eighteen, and her younger brother Gavin, fifteen.]

GAVIN: What did grand-dad *do* with all these?
CATHY: He read them of course.
GAVIN: But it must have taken him ages. I mean, it's so much easier to press a button and extract the vital information you need.
CATHY: That's just it. His generation were after something else.
GAVIN: Oh. And what was that?
CATHY: The whole thing, and not just the juicy bits. Knowledge, you might call it.
GAVIN: What difference does it make?
CATHY: I suppose it's partly a question of pace. Take that poem you did at school the other day—in your Nostalgia lesson.
GAVIN: What? [Reading it out in the most pedestrian fashion.]

'I wander thro' each charter'd street,
Near where the charter'd Thames does flow

And mark in every face I meet
Marks of weakness, marks of woe.'

CATHY: That's the one—though you've disguised it admirably. Well, in his day, you see, this would have been in an 'English' class, and you would have had to interpret it.
GAVIN: You mean, do all the donkey work myself?
CATHY: Exactly. You couldn't just press a button on the computer like we can, and—hey presto! there's an instant drab translation:

'I ponce about a city run by Mr Big, and see nothing but hassle wherever I go...'

GAVIN: Now that's a language I can understand.
CATHY: No, you had to look at it line by line, see how the poet achieves his effects, study the patterns of imagery.
GAVIN: You mean, all that 'mind-forg'd manacles' stuff.
CATHY: It's called poetry, Gavin.
GAVIN: But what practical purpose does it serve?
CATHY: Oh, 'practical'. It's a question of aesthetics: the manipulation of language, converting the mundane into the beautiful.
GAVIN: All I know is, no one writes poetry any more, so it can't have been worth doing in the first place.
CATHY: It's out-of-date, you mean?
GAVIN: Yes, like... classical music.
CATHY: You're pleased, aren't you, that they've finally scrapped Radio 3?
GAVIN: But if less than 5 per cent of people listen to it...
CATHY: You're just quoting the controller. And about the same percentage go to university, don't they? But I'm one of those people. Is my opinion not worth considering? [Pause.] Well? You see, Blake isn't as dated as you think. These 'mind-

forg'd manacles' are still going on. The minority—worse, the individual—is being stamped out.

GAVIN: You know, you sound as reactionary as grandfather.

CATHY: 'Reactionary'? Where did you get that from?

GAVIN: I don't know. It just came out. You must admit, you've got a chip on your shoulder.

CATHY: And that's the final straw: even our clothes are computerised.

GAVIN: Well, you will wear the Mike Roe label.

CATHY: If I wasn't such a frump in Armani.

GAVIN: But it's great: no more butter-fingers: your sweetheart points the zapper and your zip comes undone.

CATHY: Gavin!

GAVIN: Let's face it, Cath, you're as techno-crazy as I am, you're always on the internet to that friend of yours in Australia—you can convey messages to each other in seconds. In the old days she'd have been your... what did they call it?... 'pen-friend'?

CATHY: [sighing] I'm not saying it's all bad. Obviously things are less primitive than they used to be. I just think that with all these advances in technology, at the same time we're in danger of regressing. I mean, look at these books we've been sorting out—why do you suppose they were written?

GAVIN: For money?

CATHY: Cynic. Don't you think these writers must have felt the need to express something about the world they lived in? And the reason books are a thing of the past is that we have nothing more to say.

GAVIN: We know it all. Besides, we don't have the time for such luxuries.

CATHY: It's shameful. Though everything's made easy for us, stored away on computer, we're all in such a hurry, there's never a moment to celebrate ... It seems to me we live much longer, but appreciate far less. Even longevity itself.

GAVIN: Sorry?

CATHY: They used to get letters from the Queen, you know.

GAVIN: Who did?

CATHY: People who reached a hundred. Now it's so

commonplace, no one would bother, even supposing there was still such a thing as a monarchy.

GAVIN: Long live the Republic.

CATHY: And talking of centenarians, don't you think Blair's become just a little blasé?

GAVIN: Well, it is his eleventh term, and canonisation didn't help.

CATHY: Yes, making it presthumous like that ... It's hard to believe there was ever such a thing as a Tory government. Only going through grand-dad's things, flicking through his library at my leisure—and this year off is perhaps the last leisure I'm to know—I'm rediscovering the past. Books are our heritage—literally so, in one case. I mean, did you ever read the book he wrote? [She picks up a copy of *Second-Hand Books: a First-Hand View*.]

GAVIN: What? That dusty old thing? I've dipped into it several times, but I can't for the life of me ... You know, in some ways I was very fond of grand-dad, but you must admit, he was a bit of an old grouch.

CATHY: That's putting it mildly. But his book's well worth a read despite that—because of it? Don't forget, it was a best seller in its day.

GAVIN: That may be. Who reads it now, though?

CATHY: Oh now, now, now. That's the trouble with our generation: they can only see what's in front of them.

GAVIN: Whereas you've got eyes in the back of your head?

CATHY: Well... metaphorically speaking. [He shivers.] Are you *so* allergic to imagery? [Musing.] Yes, he practically retired on the profits from that book.

GAVIN: It's hard to see what all the fuss was about.

CATHY: Oh I don't know. I haven't got to the last chapter yet, but so far I've found it amusing, not to mention informative. There you are. Good old information.

GAVIN: Yes, but what about? Books. What use is that to anybody?

CATHY: The trouble with you, Gav, is you're a philistine.

GAVIN: What sort of book is it anyway? I mean, I could understand if it filled a particular niche.

THE FUTURE OF THE BOOK

CATHY: 'Niche'? Since when did you use words like 'niche'?

GAVIN: Oh come on, Cath, haven't you realised by now that we're not real people, we're just puppets within the author's control, mere mouthpieces spouting out stuff he wants us to, to make some laboured point about the younger generation and the future?

CATHY: I suppose so. Only I was enjoying my role as defender of the faith so much, I'd somehow forgotten.

GAVIN: Well, don't get too carried away. Now where were we? Oh yes. I mean, I could understand if it filled a particular niche. [Pause.] Come on, do I have to prompt you now? I'm feeding you a *line*. That's cue for you to explain the author's exact intentions, just in case the reader is as baffled as I'm pretending to be.

CATHY: Oh yes. Well, the clue is in the title. It's not simply another boring old price guide, out-of-date before it even comes off the press, and it's not yet another book on the subject of collecting, nor indeed a mere bookseller's autobiography. Least of all is it a humorous stocking-filler.

GAVIN: Right. All you've done is say what it isn't.

CATHY: Let me finish. If it isn't any *one* of these things, it's all of them (and many more) rolled into one.

GAVIN: You sound like an ad for a household appliance.

CATHY: Please. It's a 'view', a panorama even, of the whole subject. It deals with the function of the book; the nature of buying, selling and collecting; the experience of auction houses, private libraries, and book sales; it discusses all kinds of books, the desirables and the undesirables, even taking the point of view of one; it gives us not only the life of the bookseller (complete with customer relations) but the afterlife as well—

GAVIN: So?

CATHY: —it's about people as well as books, human idiosyncrasy—

GAVIN: Something he *did* know about.

CATHY: —and in its encyclopaedic sway it takes on every form—essay, short story, fantasy, dramatic dialogue—even concluding (I realise now) with a critique, a built-in self-analysis, as if to pre-empt the work of the reviewer. Now that's what I call thorough.

GAVIN: But is it fiction or non-fiction?
CATHY: Does it matter? You've obviously not read any books from that period. [Gavin smirks.] All right, any period. About the time of the millennium there was a kind of shake-up in literary form: you had books with male and female versions (*Dictionary of the Khazars*), books with two stories back to back (*Happenstance*), novels that were more like biographies (*Flaubert's Parrot*), and biographies that were more like novels (*Kiss and Tell*). Placed in that context, perhaps you'll begin to understand.
GAVIN: But isn't that just a lot of literary obfuscation?
CATHY: There you go again. 'Obfuscation'. You're only fifteen.
GAVIN: Don't change the subject. I've already told you we're not real.
CATHY: Well, if we're not real, why should I bother to explain it to you?
GAVIN: Why indeed? The guy's a fraud, a confidence trickster.
CATHY: Who?
GAVIN: The author. This... O.J.M. Davis, our putative grandfather—yes, 'putative'. By the way, I have it on good authority that he doesn't even have any children, let alone grandchildren.
CATHY: Whose authority?
GAVIN: Mine. His. We *are* the author, remember?
CATHY: But that's poetic licence.
GAVIN: So not only is it fiction and non-fiction, it's poetry now as well as prose.
CATHY: I don't know what you mean. I mean, you don't know what he means. And... as to what I mean—
GAVIN: That's anybody's guess.
CATHY: You've confused me, that's all.
GAVIN: This is a smokescreen. He's simply obscuring the fact—
CATHY: 'Obfuscating' was better.
GAVIN: *Listen* to me. This book is a hotch-potch, it tries to be all things to all men—

CATHY: And women.
GAVIN: Aren't we *post*-post-feminist now?
CATHY: Where does that leave us?
GAVIN: No idea. Look, it's supposed to be funny, and yet it's clearly trying to say something 'significant', and in my opinion it doesn't do any of these things, frankly it's a mess.
CATHY: Look, Gav, maybe you are supposed to take on the role of devil's advocate, but I'm sure you're not meant to go that far.
GAVIN: And why ever not? So he can't bear to hear a dissenting voice, not even his own. That's *sad*.
CATHY: I think you just have to accept that books can be part-fiction, part-faction, it was all the rage then, he didn't want to write a series of dry, monotonous essays, he went for a more varied approach.
GAVIN: You mean, while some bits are dry, others are merely monotonous.
CATHY: [closing her eyes] Please. For example, side by side, the short story and the essay have the effect of reinforcing each other. On the one hand, by entering the imaginative world of the collector you delve deeper, bring out the humanity, start to empathise—
GAVIN: In that case, why have the general chapter at all?
CATHY: —on the other, not all collectors are the same, their areas of interest differ hugely, there is a danger in being *too* specific.
GAVIN: You've always got an answer, haven't you?
CATHY: That's not surprising, is it, if I represent the author?
GAVIN: Especially if he can control the argument, putting convenient words in my mouth, then in yours, it's all very self-indulgent.
CATHY: But Gav, that was the whole point in writing a book—I mean, if one didn't have fun in the process...
GAVIN: [shaking his head] If you think *I'm* enjoying this.
CATHY: Oh *you*. Well, it would help if you read it, not like some publisher, not just a sample here, a sample there... taking the piss, I call it.

THE FUTURE OF THE BOOK

GAVIN: He's using you again, you know that, don't you, to take a side-swipe at publishers?
CATHY: So? Do you like them any more than he does... sorry, than I do? Go on. Read it through—from beginning to end. You might enjoy it. It's about time you read a book instead of playing around on your computer all day. And when it's not that it's the telly.
GAVIN: Ah! We're back in character, I see. The children of the future. Do you suppose we'll still have television then?
CATHY: Now who's changing the subject? Read-that-book!
GAVIN: OK. Only, if I don't like it, can I put it with this pile on the floor here, that's to say, the other books of grandfather's we're going to sell?
CATHY: If that wasn't the *clumsiest* exposition.
GAVIN: Sorry.
CATHY: And the answer is 'no'. If there's one book I want to keep, it's that one. Which reminds me: where are we going to sell the others anyway?
GAVIN: You mean because there aren't any second-hand bookshops any more?
CATHY: Still a little stilted... yes, that's exactly what I mean. As no one ever bothers to read anything except off a screen—
GAVIN: —and don't forget the irony: booksellers' catalogues are confined to this space now—
CATHY: —which is catch-22, since the inveterate surfer can't be bothered with books—
GAVIN: —and the bibliophile won't be caught in the net—
CATHY: —as this generation of ours has an attention span of approximately five seconds, they're being forced underground.
GAVIN: Perhaps we can flog them at some car boot sale.
CATHY: But we don't have a car.
GAVIN: Surely our parents—
CATHY: We don't have any parents either.
GAVIN: Yes. Why is that? All we've got is a grouchy ex-grandfather, what's wrong with a couple of lousy parents?
CATHY: They don't fit, that's why. This is a skit on the generation gap, and that gap's considerably wider if it's two

gaps instead of one. Besides, you wouldn't talk so disrespectfully about your own father's book, it wouldn't be realistic.
GAVIN: Since when was this chapter realistic?
CATHY: You're splitting hairs. Besides, as you say, O.J.M. Davis doesn't have any children, and if he hasn't any children, *we* haven't any parents.
GAVIN: If we haven't any parents, how do we have a grandparent?
CATHY: Since when was this chapter realistic?
GAVIN: That's my line. We're going round in circles.
CATHY: The last of his 'digressions', I suspect.
GAVIN: [muttering] The whole book's a digression.
CATHY: Where were we? Oh yes—read this blasted book. From cover to cover. And try to pay attention... for more than five seconds.
GAVIN: OK. Here goes. [Frowning] 'Introduction: What is a book for?'
CATHY: Not *aloud*.
GAVIN: [mumbling one word at a time] 'A good book is the precious life-blood of a master spirit, embalmed...' Christ, talk of embalming, I think grandfather must have been treated at birth.
CATHY: What did I say about five seconds? You can't manage it, can you?
GAVIN: But it's so stuffy.
CATHY: He's *quoting*. Besides, it gets a lot better.
GAVIN: That sounds familiar.
CATHY: Read it—for the family.
GAVIN: Will families exist in the future too?
CATHY: Only when it's convenient.
GAVIN: Maybe I'll concentrate better on the toilet.
CATHY: Anything.
   [Gavin goes to the toilet with his copy of the book.]
GAVIN: [with a slight echo] 'There have always been readers, if only casual ones, and not classical scholars like...' Like, this is so tedious. Rupert, Rupert, Rupert.
CATHY: Rhu*barb*.
GAVIN: Heh, what's this bit here? '... am an attendant

parasite...'? He's such a crap writer he's left out the personal pronoun.

CATHY: It's a literary allusion.

GAVIN: So what allusion is he under?

CATHY: That's *de*lusion. It's a parody... of a parody: from *Prufrock*.

GAVIN: *Prue's Frock*? Another book, you mean? How can I read a book that refers to other books, none of which I've read?

CATHY: [under her breath] You're not the ideal reader, it's true.

GAVIN: What's that?

CATHY: [aloud] I don't think grandfather had you in mind when he wrote it.

GAVIN: You mean he wasn't feeling randy... I'm not surprised.

CATHY: Don't be disgusting. And that's another thing I've noticed recently. Lots of drawings of naked girls on your computer.

GAVIN: Well, I am fifteen, what do you expect? Besides, it's not me, it's the mouse.

CATHY: Just read, why can't you?

GAVIN: Oh no, not another quote. Who's Louis MacNiche?

CATHY: Mac*Neice*.

GAVIN: What's this supposed to mean: '...the drunkenness of things being various'?

CATHY: [under her breath again] You'll know about that, too, soon enough. [Aloud.] Let me explain.

GAVIN: Hold on. I'll just finish off... Ah!!!

CATHY: Find a passage you like?

GAVIN: You could say that. [Pause.] Oh shit!

CATHY: What is it?

GAVIN: We've run out of loo paper.

CATHY: What? I thought I bought a packet last week.

GAVIN: Didn't I tell you? Micro took a roll and unravelled it all over the garden.

CATHY: Even the dog's watching too much telly! Look, I'll just nip out to the corner shop.

GAVIN: But there aren't any corner shops in the future.

CATHY: [clicking her fingers] Damn! I'll have to go all the way—
GAVIN: I can't wait that long.
CATHY: What are we going to do?
GAVIN: What am *I* going to do?
         [Sinister pause.]
CATHY: Oh no... that's so contrived!
GAVIN: You must have seen it coming; I did, as soon as I was sent to the toilet.
CATHY: Aren't you the clever clogs!
GAVIN: Can you see any other alternative?
CATHY: Just make sure you use the rear endpaper.
GAVIN: OK. Here goes. [He screams.]
CATHY: What is it?
GAVIN: But if it isn't... am I seeing ghosts?... grandfather!
         [Making my entrance again with my usual glare.]
O.J.M.: Don't even think about it.
GAVIN: But it's an emergency.
O.J.M.: Over my dead body.
GAVIN: Aren't you dead already?
O.J.M.: Numb with grief, I see. Bloody kids! Why on earth did I bother?
GAVIN: But you didn't. I'm just a delusion.
O.J.M.: *Ill*usion.

* * * * *

Reader, I harried him.